I0429099

Be a Prepper

A Beginner's Guide to Surviving Disasters

Macallister Anderson

Copyrights

All rights reserved.© Macallister Anderson and Maplewood Publishing. No part of this publication or the information in it may be quoted from or reproduced in any form by means such as printing, scanning, photocopying, or otherwise without prior written permission of the copyright holder.

Disclaimer and Terms of Use

Effort has been made to ensure that the information in this book is accurate and complete. However, the author and the publisher do not warrant the accuracy of the information, text, and graphics contained within the book due to the rapidly changing nature of science, research, known and unknown facts, and internet. The author and the publisher do not hold any responsibility for errors, omissions, or contrary interpretation of the subject matter herein. All the information contained in this book is presented solely for entertainment purposes and not given as professional advice whatsoever. It is to be used at your own risk. The author and publisher cannot be held responsible for the consequences of the readers' actions. The information is provided on the understanding that the reader will use it in accordance with the laws of his or her country. References, if any, are provided for informational purposes only and do not constitute endorsement of any websites or other sources. Readers should be aware that the websites listed in this book, if any, may change.

The information herein is offered for informational purposes solely, and is universal as so. The presentation of the information is without contract or any type of guarantee assurance.

ISBN-13: 978-1523319787
ISBN-10:152331978X

MAPLEWOOD
— PUBLISHING —

Contents

Avant-Propos

Learning survival skills and what to do when a disaster or any other emergencies strike, is essential in this day and age. This beginner's guide into prepping will give you a solid starting point. You will learn what you need to know to protect yourself and your family and survive. From prepare a pantry including the food and water you will need to survive, hunkering down in your home, preparing a bug out bag and much more.

Over the past few years the prepper mentality has been spreading, with people hoarding stuff for one reason or another. There are different types of preppers out there, and the ones who normally get the attention when the term "prepper" is mentioned are the doomsday preppers.

We need to make this clear: whether you are a doomsday prepper or you are just trying to make sure that your family will not starve to death in the event of a disaster or a calamity befalling your residence, food prepping is a very important element that we must all take into consideration.

The following are reasons why our future does depend on these simple survivalist mechanisms, and why being a prepper might be the best decision you ever make:

Organization

It takes a lot of time and preparation to get your prepper's pantry in order. From the time you start planning it, through stocking all the way until you get to a position where you have to use it, you need to be organized to see this through.

Besides, you need to be disciplined enough to keep rotating food in the pantry all through the year. This kind of organization will easily flow into other avenues in your life, and before you know it we can have a population that is well aware of what goes on around them, and what to do in the event of an emergency.

Preparation

What happened in the course of and after Hurricane Katrina was a good example of why we need preppers amongst us. Generally a city will have food supplies that can and will last up to three days. Preppers, on the other hand, often have food supplies that can last anywhere from 6 to 24 months. In the event of a disaster, if we have more preppers amongst us, we will be able to survive long enough to rebuild the town after the disaster.

Independence

When you are prepping your food, you are an independent supplier and consumer of your food. Therefore, when disaster strikes, you need not worry about uncontrollable elements like taxes because you will basically be living off the normal grid, free of the stress and worries that are inflicted upon society by governments and large business corporations after satisfying their own personal greed.

Crime-free

One of the other things that preppers do is to get ready for a security breach. In the event of a disaster there will be individuals who were not prepared in advance. Faced with dire circumstances, some of these individuals will try to sneak in and steal others' foodstuff.

Preppers generally learn to be ready for such intrusions, and have mechanisms in place to deal with them. Petty crime will therefore be one of the last things you will need to worry about.

Let's get started and be a prepper!

Macallister A.

Why Be a Prepper?

A prepper is more than someone who is preparing for a major catastrophe. A prepper is also someone who is looking to make sure that they can actually survive the effects of such a catastrophe.

Preparedness is critical in today's world. If you are not prepared for a major catastrophe, then you might not be able to survive a major disaster.

What Are We Preparing For?

Preppers are people who prepare for all sorts of serious problems. These include such risks as:

- A major natural disaster like an earthquake, hurricane or flood
- Chemical-based disasters like a nuclear meltdown, chemical attack or even nuclear war
- Social collapse due to a lack of critical resources
- Economic collapse due to deflation, hyperinflation or a depression
- A pandemic involving a particular disease

The threat of what could happen during any of these situations can be very dramatic. If you are a prepper, you may have an easier time figuring out what you have to do in order to survive a particular situation.

Possible Devastating, Unforeseen and Uncontrollable Scenarios

Usually known as WTSHTF (when the shit hits the fan) scenarios, these occur when the worst possible situation materializes. There are many possibilities, just to name a few examples:

- A massive earthquake could destroy the infrastructure of a local community.
- A chemical attack on a local area could cause the spread of all sorts of dangerous conditions such as a plague, anthrax, botulism, Ebola or SARS.
- Population overgrowth could lead to an extreme lack of resources in the future. These include the resources needed for survival.
- Traditional currency, particularly paper money, may become worthless over time. This could be due to hyperinflation or a depression.
- An asteroid could strike and cause devastation by wiping out an area that is tens if not hundreds of miles in size.
- Major weather cycles that entail a prolonged drought lasting for several years could cause food supplies to die out.

Preppers prepare for these situations because they know that they are real problems that could happen. Just because it sounds unlikely does not mean that everyone is going to be totally safe.

Real Disasters

There have been many real disasters that have caused the disruption of society as a whole. These include disasters that have prompted people to survive on their own:

- The Bosnian War from 1992 to 1995 caused thousands of Bosnians to be barricaded in their own country without any protection from the government. They were forced to live on their own for an extended period of time.
- Hurricane Katrina in 2005 is considered to be the worst hurricane in American history. Much of the American Gulf Coast was forced to live on its own amid chaos from a destruction of properties, flooding and the general inability of key government agencies to actually show up to help.
- The country of Zimbabwe experienced hyperinflation in the latter half of the 2000s. Hyperinflation was measured at about 89.7 sextillion percent in 2008 – That's 89.7 with 20 zeroes after it!

These are just a few real disasters that have forced people to become preppers. Whether it is from a natural disaster, economic failure or war, or the government's threat, disasters can occur. Being a prepper is clearly the best thing for you to do in order to survive.

Are you Ready to Be Ready?

The best preppers are the ones that know what they need to do in order to survive in various societies and devastating situations. If you want to be a prepper then you have to get yourself ready before you collect all the necessary resources for survival.

A Prepper's Mindset

A prepper has a mindset that is particularly kept with care. A prepper will be someone who is:

- Accepting of lifestyle changes of all kinds, including ones that you would be forced into
- Devoted to the art of prepping and willing to adopt all sorts of standards
- Ready to be at it on a moment's notice; sometimes a disaster can come right out of the blue
- Willing to let go of technology; after all, it is not like technology is going to be open and available during a disaster
- Willing to learn all sorts of key skills related to one's survival

Types of Preppers

Not all preppers are alike. There are many different kinds of preppers, and the following are a few examples:

Off-Grid

An off-grid prepper is someone who grows their own food, has a reserve property and may even get their energy through solar power, among other non-traditional methods.

Bug-Out

A bug-out prepper is someone who has a space that one can get into in the event of a disaster as well as the many materials needed during an evacuation. This prepper will often have such things as a shelter or an alternative property to be on and plenty of survival materials that are stocked at such a property or can be quickly transported as needed.

Camping Nut

A camping nut will prepare by setting up plenty of camping materials and by learning about how to survive in the wild. This includes learning about hunting, fishing and gathering.

Hunting Nut

A hunting nut is similar to a camping nut but places a bigger emphasis on hunting for food. Much of this involves the use of traps in hunting. Knowledge on how to prepare the food after it has been caught is also a necessity.

Economist

An economist prepper is someone who invests in precious metals and raw goods on the commodity market. This is with the belief that they will actually be worth something in the event of an economic collapse where the traditional money that people have will no longer be worth anything.

Funding Your Prepper Lifestyle

It clearly costs money to get all this stuff for a prepper lifestyle, but funding the lifestyle is not hard to do if you understand what you are looking to get out of it.

- Selling items that may not be necessary can be useful. For instance, if you have some technology or other old items that may not be used now and certainly won't be used during a disaster, you can always sell them.
- Creating a safe deposit space that includes enough money to live off of for an entire year or two is always a good idea. Take a look at your general living standards and what you might expect to require during an emergency and secure one or two years of that money in your account; you may want to consider buying commodities with some of this too.
- If you are looking for added money but have nothing to sell, then getting a second job might be important as it will provide you with a little extra money for taking care of your expenses.

Sound Body and Skill Sets

A prepper must also be physically fit and capable of taking in whatever might come around in the event of an emergency. There are many body and skill sets that a prepper must hold in order to be successful when it comes to preparing for the worst possible scenario.

Physical Fitness

A person who is physically fit to be a prepper will be someone who exhibits all of these particular characteristics. A person like this:

- Is of a normal weight; anyone who is overweight will have a lower chance of surviving in the wild
- Has strong arm muscles; lifting is often required as a prepper due to the heavy nature of some of the materials being used
- Has plenty of endurance; that is, the person should be able to run and move around without becoming easily tired
- Does not hold any dependencies; for example, someone who enjoys smoking should quit.

Key Skills

A prepper should also be someone who is able to:

- Cook foods on one's own
- Understand how to store food for later use
- Grow one's own food
- Provide medical care at an intermediate level

- Use the right communicative tools, including a ham radio
- Identify different weather patterns

All of these aspects are important when it comes to being a prepper. The best preppers are the ones that have the most knowledge on what one needs to survive in the wild or in any other serious situation.

Get Ready and Cover the Basics

This chapter is all about what you should be doing in the event of an emergency. This includes a look at how you can use all sorts of plans and supplies to survive any dangerous situation that you might come across in a WTSHTF moment.

Preparedness and Emergency Plans

Are you prepared for what might happen in your local area? Here are a few pointers that you must use when setting up the best possible emergency plans.

Identify Potential Risks and Hazards

There are many potential threats that may occur in your local area. While it is true that a chemical attack, asteroid collision or governmental or economic failure can occur in practically any part of the country, you need to be aware of the specific risks that could happen **specifically where you live right now.**

Think about a few pointers:

- How often do tornadoes come around your area? How strong are they and when do they occur?
- Is your area prone to hurricanes and other massive tropical storm systems? How much of a risk is there for a massive storm to cause serious damages where you are?
- Take a look at how the drainage or rain collection features in your area are. Is there a risk of flooding?
- How far are you from a nuclear power site? These zones can be extremely risky.
- Check your local area with regards to different fault lines. Is your property in a space that is at risk of serious damage from an earthquake?

Create Emergency Escape Plans

You should set up a series of emergency escape plans for when you might have to get out of a space. Many emergency escape plans should be set up, with points relating to the following:

Escape Routes

Take a look at your local area and see what escape routes are open. Check on routes based on how busy they might be and whether they are designated by the government or other entity in an area as official escape routes.

Make sure the escape route you plan is clear and easy to use. You might want to use two or three alternate routes just to be safe.

Checklists

Make sure the right items are listed on your emergency escape checklist. Your listing should include details on:

- Anything in your bug-out bag (we'll talk about this in a bit)
- Family identification items
- Documents like tax papers, insurance documents and even computer backup materials
- Money of all sorts
- Medical items, including enough things for first-aid and for intermediate care
- Medications (if applicable)

- Food and water
- Items for preparing and accessing your food
- Sanitary materials
- Clothing
- Any items that may be used with communicating with others; bring enough batteries for all of these items too

Every item that you need when you are going to be out of your house for an extended period of time should be listed. Treat it as if there was realistic potential for you to never get back into your home. It's a tough thing to think about, but it is important to explore regardless.

A checklist should also include information on what you will have to do as you leave your property during an emergency. A checklist can include these points. This is not comprehensive, but it should make for a good start:

- Make sure the car or other vehicle you will evacuate in has enough gas and is properly maintained. You might want to get some extra gas and oil into the car just to be safe.
- Make safety materials that are left in your house easily visible. For instance, leaving hoses or chain saws out in the open for firefighters to see will help.
- Close off all items that allow air or light into your home. Shutter the blinds, seal off air vents and so forth.
- Turn off all appliances and all other electrical items inside your home.
- Leave the exterior lights on in your home to create a look as though someone is still inside the home.

Maps

Quality maps are important to have, especially since there is no guarantee you will have access to a digital map on a mobile device during an emergency.

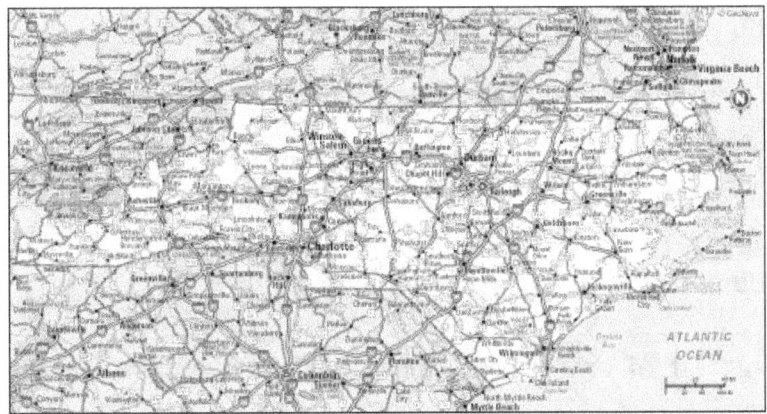

Several ideas can be used when getting your emergency maps ready:

- Look for maps that include the most recent information on where you live.
- If you can find maps that have detailed road information, then you should certainly use them to your advantage. Any type of map will work well but the best ones have as much information as possible on whatever you might want to use.
- Find maps that cover at least fifty miles of space from all directions from wherever it is you might live. If you can get anything larger, it will certainly help.

ICE Contact Persons

The In Case of Emergency, or ICE, contact list is important. This is a list of people that you can get in touch with in the event of an emergency. You can use this list to let people know where you are now, where you will be going and why you have to head out.

This listing can include the phone numbers, addresses, mobile phone numbers and even email addresses of all the people who you are going to be in touch with. If there's a way for you to get in touch with someone, then you should add it to your list.

This list of emergency contacts should include people who:

- Are trustworthy
- Live in spaces that are not likely to be impacted by the same disaster you are in; find people who are at least close enough, like a few hundred miles away or so
- Have enough resources to use to come to your aid, just in case

Involve the Whole Household and Community

You can also get other people in your home and community to join in and prepare for disaster situations. You need to particularly talk with your family members first so they will be on board with what you want to do.
You can do many things to get your household to go along with your escape plans:

- Talk about whatever concerns you might have

- Allow them to offer assistance and support on their terms
- Practice your escape plans with other family members
- Talk about how they will keep in touch in the event of any emergencies

Getting the rest of your community involved with such a plan can be a challenge, but you can do this. The best thing you can do is create a prepper group in your local community.

You can set up a community that will provide everyone with an outlet for discussing different aspects that relate to escape plans and how to prepare for emergencies. If you can discuss the threat of different disasters coming into your area, then you will certainly have an easier time getting the most out of a plan.

There are many places that you can visit when getting members for your group ready:

- Hunting stores
- Gun stores
- Farmer's markets
- Outdoorsman shops

It always helps to look online to set up groups of interest in your local area.

Test Out Your Plan

You must test your plan so you can ensure that it won't run into any problems if you have to get it going:

- Test your escape routes to see how they might run. See if you can try them out during peak traffic hours to see if they are routes that will be manageable.

- Test your carrying skills by gathering your supplies, loading them into a vehicle and getting them in as quickly as possible.

- Get in touch with your emergency contacts at a certain time to see how open they may be.

If you have others who are going to be leaving with you, see if you can get them all to meet you at a certain place with all their items before a certain deadline. If everyone can get to a space, then your plan should be rather easy to use in the long run.Build Your Emergency Supplies

Water

Water is clearly going to be very important for your survival needs. You will need to gather water for use with many pointers in mind:

Storage

- Store your water in a plastic container with a recycling symbol that has a number from 1 to 7. This is to ensure that the water will be kept safe and secure.
- A stainless steel tank can be added if you have a secure seal on it. In fact, many canteens are made with stainless steel bodies.

Purification

Purification is where chemicals and other harmful materials are removed from water.

- A portable cooker can be used to boil water so bacteria can be killed off. You'll learn more about portable cookers a little later on in this guide.
- Iodine-based tablets may be used to clean out water at room temperature.
- A water purifier can also be added to your array of water storage items. A purifier can include a UV-

based or built-in model that collects and clears out harmful impurities so your water will be clean. Some water bottles and other storage items are sold with their own purifiers.

Filtering

A water filter will create a physical barrier that your water can move through. This will cause all sorts of physical items that are in the water to be separated from the pure water, thus giving you cleaner water.

A good filter can be found on many storage bottles and tanks. It will ensure that the water is safe to drink. However, you must be aware of how you take care of the filter. A filter might have to be replaced at times or at least cleaned off. Also, the items that are collected by the filter should be cleared out on occasion.

Food

The foods that you gather can really lifesaving when you are out on the run during an emergency. Still, you have to consider the foods that you will be taking along with you.

Stockpiling and Storing Food

Make sure you stockpile the right types of foods. These include foods that can last for an extensive period of time, including:

- Whole grains
- Pasta
- Rice
- Beans
- Canned products
- Sugar
- Salt
- Nuts
- Cooking oil

Several things need to be done when storing these foods:

- Keep them in a space that is at room temperature so they will not spoil.
- Make sure everything is sealed and secured. No seals should be open on anything.
- Keep light away from all of the foods you store. Light can cause some foods to spoil.

Preserving Food

There are many ideas you can use when preserving food:

- You can start by canning your foods. You can do this by storing items in a can, placing a lid it and then adding the can into a pressure cooker with hot water to create a sturdy seal.
- A vacuum sealer may also be used to help secure all sorts of foods. This will keep oxygen atoms out of the way so the foods will not spoil very quickly.
- You can even dehydrate foods by using a traditional food dehydrator. Removing the moisture from foods will help you keep them from spoiling. You can always rehydrate foods later on if you feel the need to do so.

Drying and Canning

Drying and canning foods is not too hard to do if you understand the process.

A dehydrator is essential for helping you to take care of some of your foods, allowing you to dry off foods of all sorts. The foods can be heated at a gentle temperature that is slightly lower than what a traditional oven has. Meanwhile, the moisture in the foods will be removed, thus causing everything to be dry.

You can then store everything in a vacuum-sealed bag. Use a vacuum sealer that removes air from the bag as you close it up.

Meanwhile, the canning process requires a few important aspects:

- Use sterile cans when getting your foods ready.
- Add the proper foods that you want to store into your cans. These can include some liquids that will preserve your foods, if you want.
- Close up the cans as needed.
- Add a few inches of hot water into a pressure cooker.
- Insert the cans into your pressure cooker and seal it off.
- Bring the canner to a boil and let it vent with steam for about seven minutes.

MREs

MREs, or meals ready to eat, are field rations that may be useful for your food needs. These are packages that include a number of different foods that can make up a full meal. They are prepared by adding water and using a flameless heater that comes with the package.

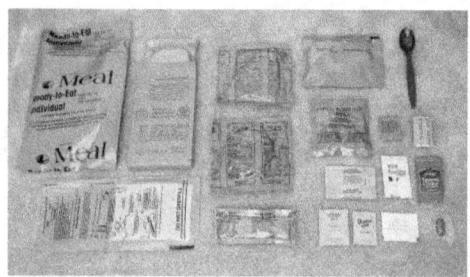

This can be ideal for your food needs, but they may not have the same flavors that you really want. Still, they can be useful if you prepare them right.

Understanding Expiration Dates

The expiration dates on foods are important to look at. These typically let you know the approximate time when the ingredients in the foods will wear out.

These expiration dates refer to when you should use items before. If you keep foods in a regular storage space for too long then they may become more susceptible to bacteria. Therefore, it is best to replace expired foods if possible so you will stay safe.

While you can use many items after their expiration dates, it is often best to freeze items if you cannot use them before those dates. Freezing foods is especially important if you have highly perishable meats.

Light, Heat and Cooking Resources

Be sure to gather the right lighting and cooking materials so you can ensure that you will not only have materials for preparing foods but also the light and heat you need to make it all work.

Light resources can include many options:

- Battery-powered flashlights can be useful.
- Solar-powered flashlights or crank-powered ones that operate with solar or kinetic energy may be useful. These often require batteries, but the battery power will not drain anywhere near as fast as usual.
- Plenty of candles and lighters are always great.

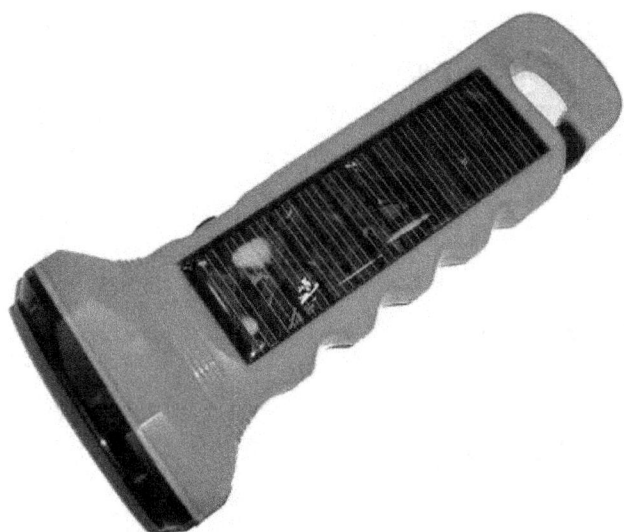

You can use some heating items too:

- A wood stove or wood pile that you can set on fire always helps. Be sure to avoid starting a fire in a flammable space, though.

- A portable propane heater can use portable fuel stores to work and start up a fire. This can be useful if you have plenty of propane fuel tanks to work with.

As for cooking, you will need a good propane heater like what appears above. This is the preferred option for heating foods in the wild as you can use a pot or other container and place it with the food inside over the heater. This can be mixed with water in many cases. If you can use a good cooker like this, you will certainly be safe.

Just be sure you have plenty of propane tanks. Propane is necessary as it will provide you with a good heat source.

Communication Tools

You must make sure to have good communication tools so you can stay in touch with others in your group during an emergency. Your tools can include the following:

- Two-way radios
- An emergency hand-crank radio

- A CB radio for a vehicle
- Traditional mobile devices, but be prepared with plenty of batteries and power adapters

Emergency Funds

Emergency funds can be useful while traveling. However, it is best to stick with the smallest bills possible. Many places may be reluctant to bring around larger bills during an emergency. Also, smaller bills should make transactions go as smoothly as possible.

You should only go for a few hundred dollars' worth of emergency funds while traveling. After all, odds are the money might not be of use if the economy collapses.

Medical Supplies

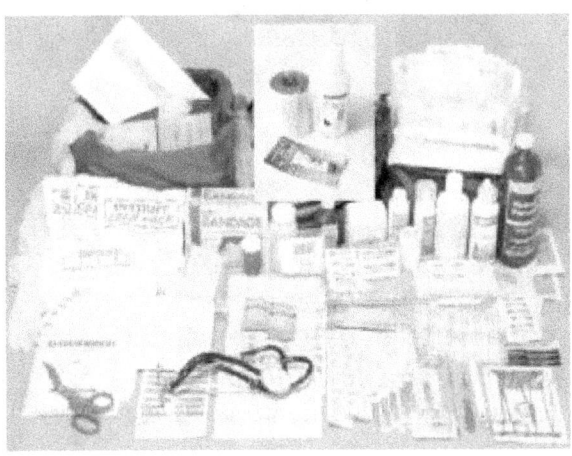

Plenty of quality medical supplies will be required during an emergency. These include such items as:

- Antibiotics
- Aspirin and other painkillers
- Stool softeners

- Slings, bandages and dressings
- Scissors to cut dressings and other items
- Sterile wipes
- Fine tweezers
- Alcohol-based hand sanitizer
- Medical tape
- Plenty of medications for whatever people need

Sanitation and Hygiene Supplies

You must also have some important sanitation supplies to keep everyone clean, as bacteria can be dangerous in many cases. You will need the following:

- A portable toilet seat with sanitary waste bags, a deodorizer and a hand sanitizer
- Toilet paper
- Sterile latex gloves
- Portable laundry soap
- A clothes line with pins to secure the line and the clothing
- Bath wipes (for when there is no way to get clean water for bathing)

- Assorted sanitary products for specific family members like diapers, incontinence products and tampons

Clothing and Temporary Shelters

Be sure to pack about five changes of clothing in your escape package to ensure that you will have enough things to wear. This is especially since you can never tell if some of your clothes will get torn or damaged.

A temporary shelter like a tent can be useful too. A tent can be propped up in any space and will create a safe haven to stay in during an emergency. It can also be useful to get sleeping bags to sleep in at night so you can stay warm and relaxed.

The Bug-Out Bag

A bug-out bag is a bag that will contain the things that you need before you flee. You will need this so you will have enough items on hand in the event that you have to leave quickly.

What Do You Need in a Bag?

There are many things you will need in your bug-out bag:

- Drinking water
- Water bottles
- Metal cooking pot
- Can opener

- Portable stove with fuel
- About two changes of clothes
- Tent
- Sleeping bag
- First-aid kit
- Survival knife
- Power charger
- Emergency radio
- Mobile phone
- Gold and silver coins
- A few hundred dollars in small bills
- A portable sewing kit

Bug-Out Bag vs. EDC Bags

An EDC, or everyday carry, bag can also be useful. It's a type of bag that contains everything you should have at all times. It can include things like a knife, some bandages, a cord or even some currency.

An EDC bag is useful but it is best to have a small EDC bag that can actually fit into your pocket. The EDC bag is supposed to be compact and should not be a full replacement for a bug-out bag.

Tips for Organizing a Bag

It will not be much of a challenge for you to organize your bag if you do a few things in particular:

- Place an emphasis on items that have many uses. For instance, a spork is better than a fork and spoon.

- Use containers to store small items so they won't roll around the bag.
- Use waterproof containers when storing items.
- Place the items that you will need to access first in the easiest-to-access spaces in your bag.
- Make sure all items that go together stick together as needed. For instance, first-aid items should be in the same first-aid kit.

Securing Your Supplies and Personal Defense

How to Secure Your Home

There may be some cases where you have to secure your home in the event that you cannot actually leave your home during an emergency. It will not be hard for you to stay safe if you are careful.

- Make sure you have plenty of outside lights to deter people from trying to get into your home. You can use solar-powered outside lights, for instance.
- Add metal grates to your windows so they will be harder to get into.

- Install prickly plants and shrubs around the home to deter people from getting in.
- Use metal doors around your home, as they are harder to break down or damage.
- Use a see-through fence around your home instead of a solid one so it will be harder for intruders to hide themselves.

WTSHTF Safety Tips

These tips will help when you are dealing with the initial threats that can come about after a WTSHTF situation:

- Make sure no one panics, or else things will be harder to manage.
- Be aware of the issue before acting upon it.
- Take care of those who are closest to you first.
- Look to see if there are any unfamiliar people who have gotten into your home and make sure you can get them out as soon as possible.

Firearms and Other Personal Defense Tools

Firearms can be used for your protective needs. You can use guns of all kinds as well as knives, or traps can be placed around your yard.

However, you need to be careful when getting your items ready.

- Make sure you have a license for firearms and that you are in a place where you can legally own them.

- Always be sure that any firearms or weapons you have are stored in spaces where no one else is going to be able to touch them.
- Look to see if certain traps are allowed for use on your property before installing them.
- Have some holsters ready for use so you can hold onto your firearms and conceal them.
- Be sure to sharpen or clean out any defense tools you might have so they can keep on working as needed.
- Don't forget to use mace or pepper spray to stop people in their tracks; fending people off is always preferred.
- Remember, do not attack anyone with a knife or firearm unless there is no other way to get someone out of a space. This is especially important if the attacker or intruder is a potential threat to your life or to the lives of anyone else where you are.

Evacuation and Bugging-Out

When Should You Evacuate or Bug-Out?

There are many signs that you should be aware of when getting ready to bug-out. You can tell you need to evacuate a space or bug-out when:

- People in your area start to buy loads of emergency supplies.
- The police or military presence in your area is increasing.
- There are massive lines at a bank for withdrawing money.
- The lines at gas stations are very long.
- Most importantly, if the local government tells you to get out then you should do so with no questions asked.

Choosing Your Bug-Out Location

A good bug-out location will help keep you and all others in your party safe and sound. You must use a few considerations when choosing such a location.

- Choose a space that is easy to get to.
- Look for a place that is appropriate to be in with regards to your skills. For instance, if you have good hunting skills, then it will be fine to choose a bug-out space in a forest that animals may be found in.

- Consider how you can use the land to your advantage. This includes using that land for growing crops or raising livestock.
- Look for a natural water source in the area.
- Look for spots that can work as shelter spaces. A cabin, trailer or other type of building can be useful if it is not in use.

What to Have in Your Bug-Out Location

Here are some things that you need in your bug-out location:

- A natural source of water
- Soil that you can grow food in
- Access to roads, preferably ones that are close to your property but won't directly link to it
- Enough space for sunlight; this works if you have solar-powered items to work with
- Wood and other items to start fires with
- Enough of a space to provide you with an escape route in the event that the location is no longer useful

Pros and Cons of Evacuation Centers

While evacuation centers can be essential for your safety in the event that you have to get out of your home, they are also problematic. These centers can be useful spaces for lots of people in the event of an emergency but you must be aware of some pointers with regards to these places.

Pros

- Capable of handling hundreds or thousands of people
- People can receive food, water and shelter
- Everything takes places indoors in a controlled environment
- Showers and electricity are available
- Full medical treatment is available

Cons

- These spaces can be crowded
- Some diseases can easily spread in such places
- There may be a limit on how many resources are available
- Not all needs may be met by such a space
- There is no guarantee that the government or any other organization will have it all running smoothly
- People in some of these spaces may become hostile over time

Getting out on your own might be the best option for your needs so your life will be safe and under control.

Sustainable Living

Long-Term Prepping

There are many cases where you might have to consider prepping for long-term emergencies. These include instances where you might have to live off of a space for weeks or months at a time.

In fact, it could get to the point where your property may no longer be open for use, or you may never get power again. You will have to use several long-term considerations in order to survive when new food, energy or money sources are not available.

Growing Your Own Food

One thing that you can do is grow your own food. You can do this by planting seeds in the soil and by growing different vegetables and fruits as needed.

You must be aware of a few points when growing food:

- Make sure you have the right seeds for planting different foods before you get to work.
- Check the condition of the soil in your area before you start. Make sure it is healthy and safe. You might need to get some fertilizer onto a space.
- If you have a clean water source, then you will need to use it to water those plants.

You can also take care of livestock. You can harvest animal-based products like milk or eggs and then take in the meats from these animals over time.

Be sure to look for animals that you can take in and feed over time. You will need to get plenty of food for your animals so they can grow and reproduce. You might have to get some animals in the wild or from a local farm to make this possible.

Water Resources

Good water resources can be hard to find in an emergency. You need to use a few plans in regards to your water needs:

- Consider using a rain barrel that has a filter and seal inside of it. This can collect rain and clean out impurities so it can be used as drinking water.
- While a good local lake or pond can help you out, make sure that you have purifiers and filters for use when you get water from these places.
- Make sure the water you take in is from a space where the water is not going to be dangerous. If the water is from a space near a nuclear power plant or sewage treatment plant then it is best to avoid it.

Homesteading

Homesteading is a practice that entails the use of agriculture with the intention of producing cloth-based materials and in preserving food sources. It is a unique aspect of prepping for all to discover because of how versatile your life plans can be while homesteading.

Homesteading often involves the growth of cotton for fabrics that may be used and processed for later needs. However, most of this involves creating regular food sources that will last for an extended period of time.

Homesteading will often involve working as hard as possible to secure animals that can provide you with plenty of food, as well as maintaining a garden and keeping it free of diseases or weeds.

You will have to react upon the first sight of any problem that comes with such food sources; you might have to eliminate an ill plant or get rid of an animal that appears to be diseased, for instance. This ensures your property will not be at risk of serious problems that may cause your food sources or their future production to be in jeopardy.

Aquaponics

Aquaponics is a practice where you grow plants outside of a soil. In particular, you will put plants in a growing material like river stones or lava rocks and then store them in containers that hang above the ground.

The plants will then be watered by a system that administers water over time. This water can come from drops that are added progressively over time and will generate a consistent amount of coverage in a space.

You may be amazed at the usefulness of aquaponics:

- It uses less water on average.
- The potential for diseases or weeds to develop is minimal.
- Less energy and land space is used.

You will have to get a number of items for your garden before you can start it up, though. To make it all work you'll need the following:

- A series of boxes to add the soil or other growth items in
- Pipes to administer water withdrawing
- Spouts that will let water come out drop by drop

Alternative Power

Alternative power is a necessity because it can be tough to get power when you are out in the wild if you only rely on traditional sources. You can typically choose solar, wind or hydroelectric power for your needs. Each option has its own features that are worthwhile.

Solar

Solar power involves the use of solar cells that are attached to a battery. These cells take in energy from the sun's rays and power up the battery so an item can work for a certain period of time.

Wind

Wind power Is where a battery is linked to a windmill. The kinetic energy is created by the windmill as it takes in the wind. This energy moves to the battery.

Hydroelectric

Hydroelectric power occurs when water moves through a generator and creates kinetic energy. This often comes from water that moves downhill through a stream or waterfall.

The need to use such alternative energy methods will vary based on what is available to you. Be sure to compare the options that are available for use so you can get a better idea of what you could benefit from.

Alternative power-based generators and other small items are available from many survivalist or outdoorsman stores these days. These are spots that will treat these like camping items but they could really be to your advantage during a catastrophe.

Improvised Sanitation and Hygiene System

You'll have to use some good long-term sanitation materials in order to ensure that your space for living will be clean and hygienic. There are many worthwhile tips that you can use.

Outhouse

See if you can build an outhouse in a space away from your property. A good outhouse can include a space where the waste can decompose and will not build up over time. You might want to build an extended trench around the outhouse.

Toilet Paper

Leaves, worn-out towels that are no longer of use and other lengthy paper-like items may be used as toilet paper.

Sanitizer

Be sure to gather plenty of sanitizing materials. You will need to get hand sanitizers ready in your space, but you can always use isopropyl alcohol for sanitation needs if necessary.

Emergency Barter Items

There could be a chance that you are unable to use cash in a situation. You might need to use emergency barter items.

If you have any of the commodities or precious metals that were mentioned earlier in this guide, then be sure to use them to your advantage. These products can be used in your bug-out plans to work as currency of sorts.

Be sure to keep a space reserved for all the emergency barter items you might have. You will need these to ensure you will be safe.

You can barter just about anything in such a situation. Here are a few things that will be useful to barter in particular:

- Water purification items
- Duct tape
- Sheets
- Linens
- Batteries
- Pencils
- Cords
- Coffee or tea
- Any type of fuel you might have

Just be certain that the items you barter are reserved in a space that contains items you will not have an immediate need for. This way, you aren't bartering anything you will miss.

What is Hunkering Down?

"Hunkering down" is a term that refers to settling in one location for an extended period of time. It entails a defensive position that you may have to take in an emergency.

The term "hunker down" is derived from the Old Norse term huka, which means to squat, and the German word hocken, which means to crouch down. The term was first recorded in the United Kingdom in the eighteenth century and had been popularized as a term used by President Lyndon Johnson in the 1960s as a means of telling people to stay where they are at given times.

No one wants to think about what can happen in a disaster. They do happen, however. There may also be disaster situations that may keep you from being able to get out of where you live. You have to be prepared in order to save and protect yourself and your loved ones.

Why Do People Do This?

Natural disasters

In some cases a tornado, hurricane, earthquake, or avalanche can necessitate you staying in one spot because there is no way how one can get out safely. Let's say that your community suffered from a category 4 or 5 hurricane or an 7.0 or higher earthquake. The odds are that the environment around you will be extremely dangerous, and there would be little that the Emergency Services in your area could do to help you out. You'd have to hunker down for a while.

Times of war or civil unrest

Some people must hunker down as a result of war or civil unrest. People in many parts of the Middle East, Southeast Asia, and Africa have been forced to hunker down as a result of wars. The Israel-Palestine conflict and the ongoing civil war in the Democratic Republic of the Congo are examples of this. Riots in Detroit in 1967 and Chicago in 1968 are also examples of society being out of control for some period of time. In these kinds of cases, hunkering down may be required.

Man-Made Disasters

There have been too many bomb attacks in America to be surprised anymore. The unhappy examples of Oklahoma City, Boston, and of course, NY all spring to mind. If your community is struck by a situation like these, you would have to stay put, just as the people in these locales did.

It's a Matter of Safety

Hunkering down is often the only thing that can be done in the event that there is a serious disaster where you are. It may be the key difference between life and death. You will have to ensure that you prepare yourself and hunker down after a disaster strikes no matter where you live or how that disaster occurred in the first place.

The Need to Hunker Down

What May Cause You To Hunker Down?

As mentioned previously, there are many natural and man-made disasters that can force people into situations where one may need to take shelter for an extended period of time. Each of the disasters previously outlined has its own particular dangers.

The air quality may become dangerous.

The air quality may be compromised in the event of a nuclear accident or chemical attack. The extreme pollutants that could permeate the atmosphere in such a case could force you to seek shelter.

The weather may be very dangerous.

Weather conditions cause most of us to stay put at one time or another. If a major disaster in winter caused the roads to be inaccessible and the power to be out, then you could easily be forced to depend only on yourself for an extended period of time. A generator-powered space set aside for the season is mandatory to avoid risking conditions that could be very hazardous.

There may not be any support coming by any time soon.

Support may not be available to your area for some time, including aid in the form of supplies or the ability to leave your safe spot. The odds are certainly that help will come, but until it does, you may need to take care of yourself and your loved ones.

Why Will Rescue Take So Long?

In certain instances and situations, it may take an extensive period of time for a rescue team to get to an area where a disaster has happened. This can occur for several different reasons:

- The roads may be hard to traverse due to flooding, cracking, or other problems.
- A space could have become isolated due to physical changes in an environment.
- The air quality may be too dangerous for rescuers to enter an area.
- Financial issues may also be a concern for the government to get everything ready for rescue and recovery. Usually, FEMA, the Red Cross, and others are there quickly, but we need to remember the government's slow response to Hurricane Katrina.
- A war or other conflict like those mentioned in Israel, Palestine, or the Democratic Republic of Congo could make it very hard for the proper authorities to get into a place.

Potential Outside Threats

The outside threats after a disaster can be especially dangerous. These can include:

- Air pollution

- The threat of weather conditions making an area even worse. This includes flooding or avalanche/mudslide threats.
- People being violent or turning to criminal activities
- Limited or no help from others you might ask for assistance

Home Security

It's clear that a disaster can bring out the best in society as people come together to help one another. However, a disaster can also bring out the worst in people. The desperate need to survive in such a condition and the panic that could arise can cause people to become violent. We know that some will engage in criminal acts. With that in mind, it will be best to protect yourself by using a number of security measures to keep your property safe.

Alarms

Alarms can be used in your home to alert you to an intruder on your property or even in your home. Alarms from a reputable security system should be placed around and in your home.

Alarms should entail the following:

- A series of durable, tamper-resistant sensors that go around doors, windows, and other spaces outside your home
- Possible invisible fence sensors around the perimeter of your property
- Glass breakage sensors that can go off in the event of a broken window
- A battery-powered control panel that requires the entering of a password
- Enough sensors to adequately cover your property.

Cameras

Cameras can be added to many spaces all around a property. They can be linked to a security system and may be battery-powered. Cameras can be placed around the corners, in entry spots, and at various other places outside your home.

Here are a few tips for using cameras:
- Get cameras that you know will be sturdy and durable. Don't buy cheap models that might wear out fast.

- Make sure the cameras can be visible so that people will know that you're watching them.
- If you can get cameras that you can control through a separate control center then it might help to use those.
- Make sure your cameras are battery-powered so they will keep working even if the power is out.

Fences

Fences can be added outside your property and can secure the perimeter at large. A good wooden or chain-link fence will be of great help, provided that it has doors that are properly secured. It also needs to be tall enough so that it would be a challenge for an intruder to climb over it without the risk of injury. In addition, a good fence needs support posts that go deep into the ground to ensure that the fence will not fall over or be shallow enough for someone to dig a hole under it. Happily, most of today's fences have support posts that can go one or two feet under the ground.

Locks

Locks are always important for the doors, fences, windows, and any other space outside your home. Get plenty of locks for your property to ensure your safety. You can also consider getting different key locks for separate spaces all around your home. For instance, the door to the front of your home might have a different key than the door in the back.

You may also want to get several different locks for some doors. Having locks on the knob and the body of the door plus a chain lock could be a big help.

Either way, you should replace the locks on your home every couple of years. This is to not only reduce the potential of someone breaking in but also to also have locks that are new, sturdy, and ready for anything that may come their way.

On a related note, try and see if you can get your doors reinforced. If you have fragile doors then you may choose to get new doors installed. Ones that have metal interiors will always be best, since they will make it extremely hard for anyone to break down.

Sealing Off Open Spaces

Open spaces can be dangerous in the event that the air quality becomes harmful. This is especially important if there are loads of chemicals in the air outside your property.

You can seal off many things in your home if you use the right materials. From cracks in the windows to cracks in the walls, all need to be sealed off.

- Check the insulation around your home, and make sure there are no empty spots or coverage gaps.
- Use caulk in spots where air might be coming in.
- If you see large cracks in a space like your foundation or walls, spray foam may help to seal off different materials and can harden all sorts of surfaces.
- A silicone tube can provide you with a sturdy liquid compound that can seal off windows while also fixing cracks in those windows.

Energy Needs

Many, many occurrences can take out the energy sources in a local spot. If this happens, then you need to be certain that you have equipment that you can use to take action when that happens. You can still get power to your property if you use a few sensible considerations.

Using a Generator

A generator can be a lifesaver. It is a device that will deliver power to your home even if the electrical grid to your home is off. There are many great generators that you can use, but you have to be aware of a few pointers when buying one:

What specifics should you look for?

- The number of watts it can handle; a unit with more watts can power up more appliances.
- The fuel it uses; gasoline is typically used in many generators.

- How much fuel it will use in a given time; that is, how long will it take for the generator to use up all the fuel you put into it?
- Whether or not it can be powered by batteries
- Power outlets; how many does it have?

Where will it fit in your home?

Look for a generator that can be stored in a space where nothing outside your home can hurt it. If you can find a generator that can link to a fuse box in your home then it will be ideal. Otherwise, a portable generator that can power up a few items at a time may be the way to go.

How much maintenance is required?

The fan in a generator might have to be checked on occasion. The oil may also have to be replaced in some models.

Managing Alternative Energy Sources

While a generator could work for getting energy into your home, another idea is to look for alternative energy sources before you need them. If you can power your home without using fuel or any electricity off of a gird, with solar or wind, for example, then you will be at an advantage and ahead of the game when disaster strikes.

Here is information about solar and wind options.

Solar

A solar-powered home would be perfect, as you will be taking in energy from the sun's rays. The rays will be collected by panels, usually on the roof, that will convert the energy into use for powering your home.

Solar power can be gathered in your home with these steps:

- Take a look at the total amount of energy that your home uses in a typical month. Consider getting enough panels and a solar generator that can handle that amount.
- Have some solar panels installed onto the roof of your home. Make sure they are installed and positioned by professions so that they will have the optimum exposure to capture the sun's rays.
- Get that generator connected to a fuse box or other material that will be responsible for distributing the power to your home.

This should provide you with plenty of energy to ensure that you don't have to use traditional resources. In fact, this will be of use even in safe periods and may cut down on the cost of electricity in your home.

Wind

Wind power is something that is typically collected in massive fields where huge windmills may be found. Wind turbines will be connected to these windmills and will create energy off of the kinetic force that comes with the windmills moving. This will then move the energy into a generator for powering up different sites.

There is a potential for you to use wind power in your home to make it capable of handling power the right way. Check with professionals on the legality of using it on your property, and the correct placement.

Wind power can really be essential if you use a few considerations:

- Figure out how much power you need off of a wind turbine, and order a windmill that is appropriate for it.
- Get the proper windmill installed. A typical windmill may be about 80 feet high and cost $30,000, but you may be able to find a smaller model that is not as expensive depending on where you go.
- Have your wind turbine connected to a generator or other material used to bring power out to your home.
- Look at the standards for living in your area and see if you can get this to work in your property. Not all communities will allow you to get such a material ready in your property. You might have to ask your local housing board to see if you can add it.

If you have a property that is significantly spaced apart from others, then a wind turbine may work. Otherwise, you might want to stick with solar power instead, due to the legal ramifications that may be involved. Be sure you fully understand whether wind power or solar power is the right form of alternative energy for you.

Food and Water

Storing Foods Properly

You need plenty of good foods to ensure that you and your loved ones have enough. These foods have to be stored with care. That is, you have to place them in the right containers and storage areas to ensure that they will not spoil or go bad.

- Keep them in a dark space. Excess light can cause some foods to spoil.
- Use a dehydrator to remove the moisture from some foods. This can work well for fruits, vegetables, and meats. The dehydrator will remove the moisture, which will allow the product to last longer without spoiling. You rehydrate the foods when you are ready to cook them.
- Use a vacuum sealer to store items in bags. This will keep the foods you have from spoiling due to excess oxygen.

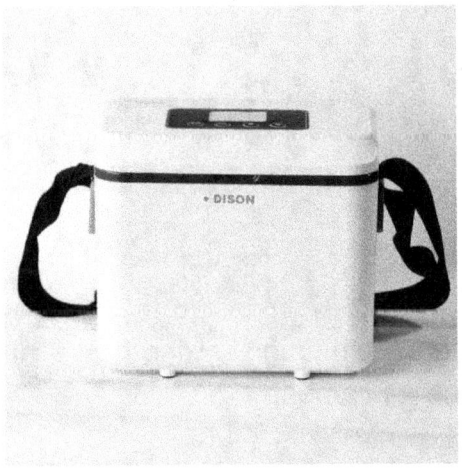

-

- If you have a freezer for perishable foods, then make sure you've got a generator to work with it. The same goes for if you have a refrigerator. In fact, a battery-powered freezer or refrigerator would be ideal.
- Of course, canned foods are the easiest since you have only to store them in a pantry or cupboard.

Preparing Your Foods

- A portable stove is vital. This will allow for plenty of heat to start up in order to cook meats and heat water among other things. You will need to get enough fuel canisters to power the stove. Fortunately, many of these cans may be used for an extended period of time before they run out.

- Also, gather enough mixing bowls and pieces of cooking equipment.

- You should get a separate space ready for a fire. A portable gas-powered grill may be useful as it does not have to be plugged in. Still, you should be certain that such a grill is placed outdoors so it will not pollute your living quarters. Doing this depends on air quality outside your home.

Finding New Foods

In the extreme case that you may run out of food, you may have to mimic your hunter and gatherer ancestors.

- Place animal traps so you can catch squirrels, birds, rabbits, and other small animals.
- If you have a garden, you must continue to take care of it, if the air and water are safe. This will give you vegetables and perhaps grains. Also have a fence around your garden to protect it.
- If you live near a water source, you'll be able to gather it there. You can also harvest water, which we will talk about in a bit.

You may have to protect yourself while outdoors. Bring along plenty of things to stay safe in the process. We will cover what you have to do if you need to go outside later in this book.

What Foods Should You Have?

- Non-perishable foods, particularly canned meats, fruits, and vegetables; foods that can last for years
- Canned soup, juice, and milk

- Dehydrated foods; this especially works for meats, fruits, and vegetables
- Salt and pepper
- Sugar
- Coffee and tea
- Water
- Peanut butter
- Granola bars

Make sure you have a non-electric can opener too. Plenty of clean water is also needed for cooking something. This leads us into the next topic for you to take a look at.

Managing Water

Water is essential to have for your survival needs. You may still have access to water supplies while hunkering down. That is because typical water supplies are often going to work even when the power is not active in a spot.

Bottled water can always be useful as it will ensure that you will have plenty of clean water for an extended period of time. You need to watch for a few things when getting bottled water:

- Look for bottles that are sturdy. The plastic cannot be flimsy or weak. Glass is even better.
- Make sure the protective seals on any bottles of water you get are screwed down tight.
- Bottled water should be used for drinking. Water you get from a tap should be used for bathing or preparing foods.
- Use plenty of filtration materials to help clear out potentially dangerous materials from your tap water.

Water bottles have expiration dates, but it's not because the sealed water will go bad. In fact, the only reason why bottled water products have expiration dates is because some states, most notably New Jersey, have laws stating that every consumable product must have an expiration date on it. This includes things that don't really expire, like water. You will see expiration dates on these bottles regardless of where you live. There is no real reason to be concerned about these dates.

Also, if you have gathered some kind of water from an outside source, or you have opened the seal on a bottle of water, then you should discard whatever is not used about a week or two after you first open it. Old water can be a breeding ground for bacteria.

Purifying Water

There is the potential that water can become dirty. This is particularly the case if you get water from a tap or from an outside source. While it is true that quality filters can help to reduce the potential for some bacteria to get in your water supply, you should always be certain that you have the right materials on hand for when you are going to purify water.

You can easily purify water if you use a few considerations:

Boiling

You can boil water to kill off the bacteria, using a portable stove.

Iodine Purification

Iodine tablets may be used in water to purify it. Iodine tablets can take a good deal of water and neutralize bacteria. This works best if the water is at room temperature. Those who have thyroid issues, are taking lithium, or are pregnant might want to avoid this method.

Purification Device

A purification device may also be used. An ultraviolet purifier can be added to water by using a pen-like material in a water supply to create UV rays that will kill off the bacteria. Meanwhile, water can be poured into a bottle and then sealed with a built-in purifier to help you clear out bacteria as it will work like a pump of sorts

Hygiene

You cannot skip on hygiene while hunkering down. Good hygiene is vital for your health. Several things have to be done in order to guarantee that hygiene can still be intact while you are hunkering down.

Bathroom Control

There is no guarantee that the water supply in your bathroom will continue to work during an emergency. If the water can work, then there's no problem. If it doesn't work, there are alternatives.

Composting Toilet

The composting toilet is a great type of product that you can use to deal with human waste. This kind of toilet will be attached to a deep space where human waste can move into. The space will be designed to facilitate the decomposition of the waste and can be managed with sawdust to help neutralize odors and to facilitate the decomposition process.

Disposing of Human Waste Properly

You might also have to think about the removal of human waste if you have something like a camping toilet in the event that you don't have access to water for a traditional toilet. You will have to particularly take any human waste that is gathered by such a toilet and secure it in a bag to be moved outside.

You will have to ensure that the human waste you do dispose of is stored in a separate space that is away from the rest of the garbage. This is to ensure that the waste will not contaminate any surfaces and also so it will decompose on its own.

Sinks

The sink that you have should be checked with care as well. You might have to use a hand sanitizer in your bathroom as a means of cleaning off your hands. This is to ensure that your hands will be protected and free of the harmful bacteria that you might get over time.

Cleaning Surfaces

You will have to make sure that you clean off the surfaces in your property with care so it will not be at risk of suffering from serious problems. All of your surfaces will have to be treated well as bacteria can really spread around a surface with ease. Several things have to be done to ensure that bacteria and other harmful compounds will not get in the way of any of the surfaces in your property.

Store plenty of cleaners.

You need to use plenty of fine household cleaners in your home. Look for sink, mirror, toilet and counter cleaners. If you can use safe organic cleaners that do not create loads of fumes then you will certainly protect everyone in the home.

Get a vacuum or sweeper ready.

A good vacuum can help you out but it helps to have a sweeper that does not require power ready. A sweeper can help you to collect all sorts of items and can use pads that you can dispose of after use. On a related note, you need plenty of these pads but having ones that can be washed and re-used will be even better for you to have.

Use safe cloths for drying off surfaces.

You must also use safe cloths that are easy to manage. Anything that will not leave off a bunch of lint will help. In addition, any cloth that can be cleaned off properly should be managed with care as having a cloth will work better than having a bunch of paper towels that you might have to dispose of over time. We'll talk about cleaning off these cloths in a bit in the laundry section of this guide.

Taking Care of Garbage

You need to be certain that you understand what you want to do with your garbage when hunkering down. Several things have to be done in order to keep the garbage in your home from being a serious issue.

81

You have to use a few important tips for managing garbage:

- See if you are able to reduce the total amount of whatever you produce. Conserving what you have is critical for garbage-management needs as it will ensure that your need to manage garbage won't be much of a problem. This is especially critical as your garbage might have loads of bacteria that can bother any surface in a home.

- Check on what you are able to recycle; make sure you recycle items and use as compost for a garden if you have one.

- Reusing some items may also help you out. If you take an old water bottle and wash it out and use it for handling more water later on then you will certainly reduce the amount of garbage you will produce.

- If you do have to move garbage outside your property then you will have to make sure you move your garbage out to a space that is relatively off from your property. If you can move out to your curb then make sure you do so as quickly as possible; we will talk about what to do if you have to go outside later on.

You must especially be certain that you dispose of your garbage when it gets full. This is especially the case if you are trying to take care of a baby; you can never tell how many diapers that child is going to use.

Showering and Cleaning the Body

Laundry Work

Your laundry plans should be reviewed when you are trying to manage your live while hunkering down. You could technically have access to water during an emergency but at the same time you may not have the power you need to get a clothes washer and dryer to work for you. That's why you would have to use an alternative plan for managing your laundry.

Make sure that you are careful when getting your laundry ready. You will need to get plenty of space in your home to make it useful. You can always use the room in your home where you normally do your laundry in when taking care of the process.

In addition, you can reduce the needs you might have for cleaning off clothes; if you are able to wear something for two days then it will certainly help you out. Of course, if you become incredibly dirty or the clothes start to wear out then you will definitely have to take them off.

There are many things that you need to use in order to manage the laundry in your property:

Washtubs and Washboards

These old-fashioned utensils can be of enormous help with getting your clothes washed. They're super effective and will work without the use of any energy but your own elbow grease.

Soap

Practically any kind of soap can be used when managing your clothes this way. You could even use bar soap.

Drying Line

You can add a line onto the wall and use fasteners to secure it in its place so it will be taut. Make sure the line is not too long and that you have space for whatever you are cleaning.

__Tooth Brushing__

Toothpaste and extra toothbrushes should be on your "must have" list. Use as little of your precious water supply as possible when brushing your teeth.

What About Your Baby?

- Because you may have difficulty with the amount of garbage you produce, cloth diapers, which can washed and re-used as needed, may be preferable. You might want to get a totally separate trash bag for waste and keep it far from anything that is consumable. Better yet, dig a hole in the ground, as a kind of "outhouse."
- Reusable cloth wipes can also be used in your home when you've got to clean off your baby.
- Keep a changing and care station for the baby in a spot that is away from the food preparation area or other living spaces in your home to protect those spots.

Communication

Even when you are hunkered down and staying safe, there will almost always be potential for you to communicate with others. Using communication methods to send signals to other people increases the possibility that professional help may come to you.

Satellite Phone

The land and mobile phone networks might be out during an emergency, but a satellite phone can still help you reach others. This type of phone operates with satellites instead of regular cell sites. A satellite phone looks rather rudimentary when compared with a typical Smartphone. It has its own battery, but it will not have many features outside of the ability to call someone. You can find many satellite phones for $300 - $600. Considering how many of these phones were closer to $1000 each a few years ago, this could be a real bargain for you to use.

Weather Radio

A weather radio is another must-have. It is a battery-powered radio that will take in access to weather radio stations that are broadcast on a certain band.

If you live in the United States then you will get access to NOAA broadcasts. If you are in Canada then you can get Weatheradio Canada reports. This type of radio will keep you up-to-date on emergency conditions as they occur. Be sure to regularly listen with this type of radio.

Citizen's Band (CB) Radio

The Citizen's Band radio is an interesting form of communication that provides you with two-way connection if a phone network is not open. This helps you send signals out if you are going to try and communicate.

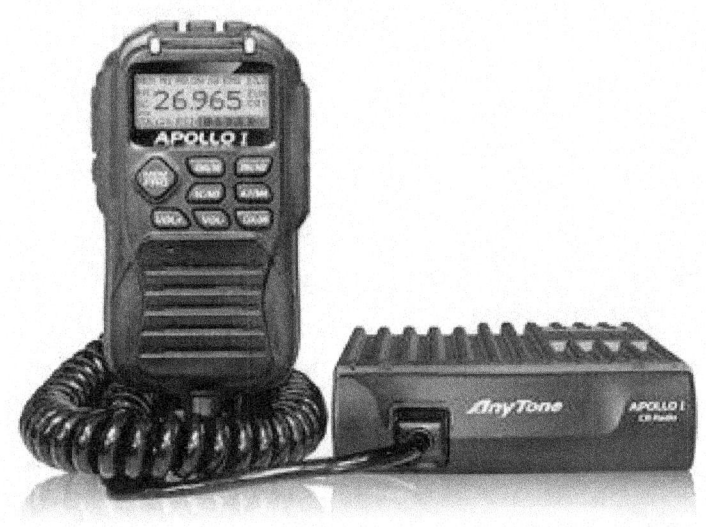

Be aware when finding a CB radio that you can also get access to different police, fire, and emergency radio signals. It's imperative that you listen to these regularly to hear what is going on and if there are any changes in conditions where you are.

Wireless Network

There is a possibility that a wireless network may still be intact when you are hunkering down, depending upon the extent of the damage in the disaster that you are getting through. If the wireless network is open, then you should be certain that your phone is charged properly. A good solar-powered charger or a battery-based charger is vital.

In addition, you might have to check and see where in your property you will get the best cell reception. This is to lower the odds of you having dropped calls.

Clothing

You will need adequate clothing in order to make it through any situation as you stay in your protected situation. Having plenty of clothing helps as it will ensure that you will be protected. A good rule of thumb would be to have about two or three weeks' worth of clothing when you are hunkering down. This quantity of clothes will also keep your laundry under control as you will not have to worry about cleaning too many items.

The types of clothing that you should have will be important to figure out. Be sure to get the following ready for when you are hunkering down:

- Jeans
- Shirts
- Jackets; gather wind jackets for the spring and heavy jackets for the winter
- Socks
- Shoes; walking shoes that fit around your feet well are the best ones to have
- Hats; this is for when you are trying to deal with hot conditions
- Shorts; this is provided that you are not going to be outside and the conditions are rather hot
- Underwear
- Long underwear, gloves and other thermal materials that can retain body heat; this is critical for the winter season

It does not matter how the clothing looks. What matters is that you have enough clothing to last for two weeks during any part of the year. Having different types of clothes for varying seasons will especially help you out.

First Aid

Adequate first aid is a must. You must be ready for cuts, bruises and other commonplace problems, as well as more serious problems. Never skip on the first aid that you plan on using.

Bandages and Splints

These are to secure cuts, broken bones, and other common concerns. Items to have, include:

- Sterile bandages
- Adhesive tape
- Folding splints
- Sterile gauze pads
- Shaped bandages - circular and triangular bandages can cover joints
- Safety pins in several sizes

Treatment Items

There are a number of good non-prescription items that you can get:

- Antacids
- Pain relievers
- Laxatives
- Eye wash
- Rubbing alcohol
- Hydrogen peroxide or any other antiseptic
- Activated charcoal
- Anti-diarrhea medicine

Also, you must have an adequate supply of any prescription medications you and your loved ones take. Be aware of expiration dates. While it is true that these are safe to use if they are fully sealed in sterile containers or packages, there is a potential for some medicines to lose their potency if they are not used within a particular period of time.

Tools

Have a good supply of these:

- Tweezers
- Scissors
- Thermometer
- Latex gloves
- Cleaning soaps
- Antiseptic spray, which may be useful for sterilizing different tools
- Razor blades
- Wooden application sticks
- Petroleum jelly or any other safe-to-use lubricant

What About Serious Emergencies?

If you have to deal with a serious medical emergency, you will probably need to get in touch with someone from outside. Next, we will cover information on what to do in this event.

What if I Have to Go Outside?

It's clear that there is the potential for the outside world to be dangerous after a disaster strikes. There may be loads of pollutants in the air, buildings could be down, looters could be out, and roads could be impassable. You certainly may not want to consider it, but the truth is, there may be times when you have to go out. These include:

- When you've got to get waste out of your home
- When there is a serious medical emergency that you cannot just treat on your property
- When you have to get supplies

You can make preparations for going outside. Some of the things you may need include:

Protective Breathing Materials

You might need protective breathing in the event that the air quality outside your home is not good. While it is true that you might get by with a typical face mask, a gas mask will cover serious problems with the air. Keep both on hand. Having goggles and ear protection are good ideas too.

What to Carry

You should carry a few important things on your body:

- Identifying information
- Any means of communication like a phone, if it works
- Something to barter with
- A proper security knife to cut through items if needed
- A bottle of water
- A portable, pocket-sized first aid kit

Signaling For Help

- Get flares that you can shoot off to get attention. Make sure the flare is bright and can be seen from a distance. Always shoot it off directly upwards towards the sky.
- A good banner sign may also be added so someone from a plane or helicopter can see it. Any banner sign that is about fifty feet long and at least ten feet wide will work. Make sure it is clear and easy to read without small print that may be hard to read from a typical helicopter.

Getting a Car Ready

You should always have you car ready. Have repairs made immediately upon needing them so that you're not in the position of requiring them during a disaster. Keep oil and all other fluids up-to-date. Keep tire pressure within appropriate limits. Keep the gas level between half and full, especially if you're in a dangerous area prone to problems. With the right car, properly serviced and ready to go, you'll be able to drive away from some disasters.

Keep these in your trunk at all times:

- An empty gas can
- A tube to be able to siphon gas
- Car jack
- A spare tire
- Jumper cables
- A spare battery

- A gallon or more of water for the cooling system, not for personal consumption
- A few quarts of oil
- A wrench for managing the tires if necessary
- Flares and signs in the event that you need to signal someone for an emergency while on the road

Assorted Needed Supplies

There are items which may not be necessary for survival but nonetheless add to our comfort and sanity, especially in tough situations. Gather these into a special box that you can pull out when you need to.

Home Comforts

It never hurts to have a few comforts for your life while you are hunkering down. These home comforts can include the following items:

- Shaving gear
- Makeup
- Liquor
- Candy and sweets
- Books
- Blankets and pillows
- Toys that don't have to be powered by batteries

Games

Board games are a great choice to keep on hand because they don't require power. Crossword and puzzle games are perfect to bring into your shelter. Games such as Charades, Twister, and 20 Questions are but a few parlor and team games you can play with your loved ones.

Recreational Materials

Having some recreational materials might help as well.

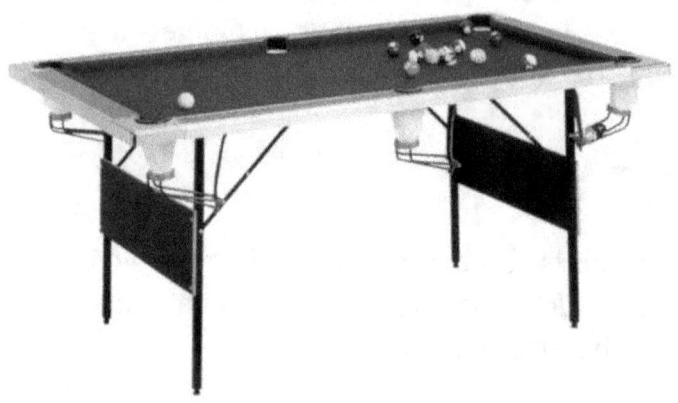

There are many things that you can have:

- A dart board
- A collapsible and portable game table may also be added. This can provide you with many games to play like pool or table tennis and can be taken apart and placed in storage when you don't need it.
- Cards to use for card games would be great too.

Food Pantry in Prepping

It is evident that food and water storage is an important part of any prepper's system. When one is preparing for any type of disaster, this is the reality. It is therefore necessary to learn about proper food storage and management and how to store and treat water for a perfect prepper's food pantry.

As you start to produce your own food, a prepper's pantry becomes his lifeline, especially during disasters. An emergency food pantry is a supply of food that your family could survive on in the event that a disaster ever cuts off your normal access to food, water and utilities. Therefore, having a well-equipped emergency food pantry is a necessity for every family. The foods should be non-perishable foods that do not require refrigeration, cooking or water. Beyond these guidelines, what you put in your emergency pantry is entirely up to you.

The process of setting aside a supply of food is a simple way of being prepared for any future emergencies. It is recommended that you store enough food and water for three days, but survivalist experts often advise to set aside provisions that will last a week to account for a worst-case scenario. In all these situations, the focus is on foods that provide a balance of nutrients, stay edible over the long run, and take up as little space as possible.

This is the best way to ensure that your family has enough food and water during an emergency. You are required to plan in advance and store rations on which you can draw if the power is out, municipal water is inaccessible, or if you cannot get to a store to buy what you need. The storing of emergency food can be more manageable if you incorporate your emergency purchases into your regular shopping routine and also store emergency rations along with your daily food supplies.

To effectively manage food supplies and become self-reliant especially in terms of disasters, a food prepper's pantry is an ideal solution. It makes sure that you are able to provide for your family when crisis strikes. Food and water are part and parcel of human survival. Without these two components, life cannot be sustainable. It is therefore prudent to come up with ways of making sure that there is continued provision of water and food, especially when things are difficult. It is critical to understand what the whole process of a prepper's pantry entails, including having a proper plan for food and water storage.

Factors to consider when Preparing Food and Water for Emergencies

It is good to plan ahead as to how you will provide food and water for your family before a disaster strikes. Disasters include fire, famine, floods, hurricanes, tornados, earthquakes, and more. The disaster could be of a bigger or smaller magnitude than you expect. The main objective of having emergency food and water supplies is to ensure that you are able to support your family's needs for a relatively long period of time. You can be in a position to manage all these by incorporating emergency buying into your normal shopping. In light of this, there are some considerations that need to be taken in mind when storing water or food for emergency use.

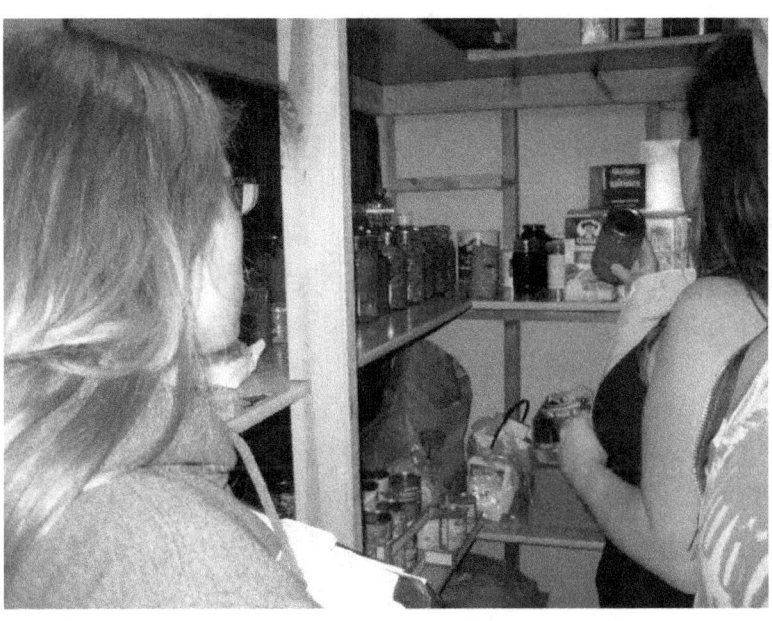

Food Storage

Nonperishable foods: The first thing you need to have in mind is that you should choose nonperishable foods for emergency rations, such canned goods, beans, cereals, dried fruits, peanut butter, rice, jerky, and jelly. You need to include a variety of fruits, meats, treats, and vegetables that your family can use without cooking.

Comfort foods: The next step is to keep foods that your family likes eating on hand in case of emergency. Familiar foods can help ease stress in such times. You should not forget favorite gravies, spices, and sauces to add variety to noodles, beans, soups, and rice dishes.

Dry foods: It is prudent to store dry mixes, flour, and cereal in airtight containers. Each of these should contain sufficient food to feed your family for one or two meals. In addition, one needs to use airtight quart canning jars in storing instant soups, powdered milk, potato flakes, and dehydrated fruits and vegetables. All containers and jars should be marked with food contents and storage dates.

Storage location: In addition, you should select a dry and easily accessible location to store your emergency food rations. Pantry shelves and kitchen cupboards are ideal. Foods should be rotated after each shopping trip to keep older foods in front and to ensure that they are to be consumed first. It is advisable to store a manual can opener with your food supplies.

Pest control: Finally, it is important to store food in an area free of pests. Insects, rodents, and other pests can chew through packaging, so you should check the pantry frequently to ensure there are no signs of any pest infestation.

Water Storage

Bottled water: One of the most important considerations in emergency water storage is to keep cases of bottled water on hand in case of a crisis. Plan to use at least one gallon of water per day, per person, for drinking, instant drink mixes and mixing with food, as well as for personal hygiene.

Tap water: The other factor is to store tap water for cooking and drinking for up to six months in clean two-liter soda bottles that have been washed in hot, soapy water and rinsed clean. Bottles should be sanitized first by cleaning them thoroughly in a mixture of four teaspoons of unscented household chlorine bleach in a gallon of water.

In addition, the bleach mixture should be rinsed out of each bottle with fresh water before being refilled with fresh tap water. If you are using well water, four drops of unscented household chlorine bleach can be added to each bottle. Stored water needs to be capped tightly and marked with the date of preparation.

It is good to remember that in order to make it easier on you, water needs to be stored in a variety of container sizes. Gallon jugs are perfect for food preparation and cleanup, but having some smaller bottles for drinking means you won't need to use glasses unnecessarily.

Besides, you might not even have the time to use the glasses, so if you can use the smaller bottles, it would be easier on you, especially if you need to move from one place to another.

Buying unopened, sealed water is one of the safest and least labor-intensive ways to store water. It can be expensive, and for this reason it is not necessary, but as long as you are willing to take the extra steps to ensure that the water is stored in a correct manner, you should be good to go.

Soft-drink bottles are considered ideal since they wash out easily, and they come in convenient sizes. However, juice or other drink containers made of PETE plastic are also acceptable. That said, it can be difficult to get all of the juice residue washed out of them. You should not use milk jugs; this is because they quickly break down and are not designed for long-term storage. Finally, the water should be stored in a dry, cool location and should be used up within no more than six months.

It should be noted that the ideal temperature for both food and water storage is between 40° and 70° Fahrenheit, while the humidity needs to be low in the storage area. This is because moisture increases the risk of mold bacteria growth and damage, as well as speeds the breakdown of packaging materials. In addition, it is also important to keep food and water supplies away from direct heat or sunlight sources. This can speed up the breakdown of both food and packaging.

Water Safety

You may be tempted to use tap water and containers to prepare water for storage. This is much less expensive than purchasing water, and you can easily rotate in the fresh supplies without any feeling of wastage. At the same time, if your water comes from a clean source, pre-treated with chlorine, as is the case of most public water supplies, you only need to put the water in clean containers for storage.

You should be sure to use plain bleach, rather than the ones with added thickeners. The water will be safe to use when needed, though it is good to rotate through the entire emergency stock of food and water once a year. This will help you ensure that you do not have any wastage or stock that will lie unused for a very long time.

In addition, it is advisable to store extra water for young children, pregnant women, the elderly, or those who are ill. This is because they may naturally need more water compared to other members of the family. At the same time, you should keep extra vegetable oil, shortening, and canned butter on hand to use in cooking.

There should be enough stock of vitamins and dietary supplements in case of emergencies. It's also good to count family pets among family members for purposes of planning how much food and water needs to be stored.

Another point to note is that one should not ration water if his supplies run low. Instead, he needs to look for additional water sources, such as the hot water heaters or swimming pools. In times of emergencies people should avoid fatty or salty foods.

These foods tend to make you crave liquids, which, as we know, are in short supply at the moment.

Basic Rules for an Ideal Prepper's Food Pantry

A lot of people make the mistake of creating a food supply that is only meant to keep their stomachs from growling in hunger. This can only help one to survive a short-term disaster. However, if a crisis situation is prolonged, you will need a food supply that feeds and nourishes the body system, not just one that keeps hunger off. You must prepare to fuel yourself for building a new, more self-reliant kind of lifestyle. If you fail to do this, you will perhaps only be able to survive for as long as your food supply is not empty.

In addition, those who plan to take the first steps in preparing for disasters may feel a bit overwhelmed as to where to begin the entire process. There is a lot of food to choose from at the grocery stores. There are many websites that encourage families to start buying small amounts of food-related preparedness items each time they go shopping. This is advisable because it allows you to prepare in advance over time without necessarily having to run panic purchases in the course of a disaster.

Besides, it is common knowledge that when disaster strikes, there will be shortages and essential items will either run out, or their prices might shoot up exponentially.

One of the tools that you will need for planning in such situations is the food storage calculator, which can help you understand how much food your family will need for a given emergency. At the same time, the food storage calculation can also be printed out and used as an inventory list to help you in keeping track in terms of what preparedness supplies you have or will need. In order to make the most of your emergency food supply, these essential food pantry rules should be kept in mind before doing you go shopping.

You can visit:
http://lds.about.com/library/bl/faq/blcalculator.htm
to get access to a food storage calculator to help you figure out what your family would need for a full year. The Latter-Day Saints created this calculator that people – even those who aren't associated with the LDS church or even any church in general – can use to help figure out what they need based on the key building blocks of one's diet that must always be utilized for survival needs. It is a very useful tool. Please note that the water supply is for 14 days as it is unpractical to store a full year of water supply.

Daily Calorie Requirements

In the event of a disaster, the ultimate goal for you is to make sure that you fend off malnutrition. You might be facing a tough time ahead, but it is equally important for you to ensure that you do not starve to death. Proper nutrition will keep you alive, strong and active enough to support yourself and your family members, or those under your care. Because of this you will need to make sure that you have the right kind of food that will support your nutritional needs. You will need to stock up on the kinds of foods that provide essential nutrients for maintaining body functions, carbohydrates and proteins, and fats for energy.

On the same note we have to highlight again the fact that your food needs to contain as little salt as possible because the more salt you have in your diet, the higher your thirst for water will be, and you might be in a situation where getting a proper water supply might be a challenge.

Multipurpose food supplies

There are a number of food items that can serve more than one purpose, helping with finances and saving precious space in the food storage pantry.

Such items include pasta, oats, wheat, rice, and beans.

High-Energy Snacks

High-energy snacks are good for boosting your energy, especially in times of emergencies. Therefore, eating snacks that are high in complex proteins and carbohydrates will be the best way to ensure that you stay stronger. In fact, high-energy snacks such as peanut butter, nuts, granola bars, crackers, and trail mix can be stored for up to one year and will help in keeping energy levels and spirits high in an emergency situation.

Proteins

Protein is an essential ingredient in our diet, and thus it cannot be omitted from the diet during times of survival. A good source of protein is canned meat, which can help you maintain energy levels. In addition, meats such as ham, chicken, tuna, and spam are also great protein sources for the food pantry. Did you know that the oil in canned meat can be used as an emergency candle?! Some other easy sources of proteins are beans and rice. Together, they make a complete protein mix, providing all the amino acids that you will need to survive.

Don't Forget the Basics

Sometimes people forget the most basic essentials, such as flour, cooking oil, cornmeal, sugar, salt, spices, baking powder, baking soda, and vinegar. These should not be overlooked. If these are present in your kitchen, they should also be in your emergency food supply. Even though during an emergency you might only use them from time to time, or not as often as you normally do, the most important thing that you have to understand is that when it comes to emergency situations, you take any chance you get as a golden chance, and utilize it.

Convenience and Variety

A lot of parents know that boxed dinners can be quite the lifesaver when you are running out of time. Thus, having some pre-packaged dinners and meals that you can grab during emergency situations will help in acclimatizing you to cooking in a grid-down scenario and also provide some comfort at the same time.

Variety, in all life situations, brings forth pleasure. This is also the case in the food pantry, where it prevents the monotony of eating the same type of food all the time. Again, it is important to mention that having well-rounded food storage in a pantry cuts down on culinary boredom and provides a balanced diet. At the same time, stocking up on a variety of spices will enhance the appeal of your pantry.

The interesting thing about planning for your pantry is that you need to try as much as you can to get a good variety in store. Lack of variety will easily breed boredom, and boredom will make it harder for you to eat the food you need to survive. This is especially so for your kids. Anything that will affect the appetite of your kids needs to be dealt with appropriately, especially because kids, unlike adults, might not really understand the dire extent of the situation at hand.

Finding Comfort in the Little Things

It is imperative that you stock some comfort food items that provide pleasure to the family. Some effective examples include sweet cereals, popcorn, juice boxes, hard candy, pickles, pudding, applesauce, and cookies. These could be a great way of providing a bit of normalcy to any emergency situation one may encounter.

Besides, some of these snacks are also a good way to boost your energy. It is therefore necessary that you try and make sure that you get just the right kind of snacks, ones that will be able to not only keep away the boredom, but at the same time keep you healthy and strong.

Backing Up Your Backup

It is indeed true that compressed food bars are lightweight. They taste good and are nutritious. You can include food bars in your pantry as a backup to your existing food supply. These could provide you some peace of mind by knowing that you have an alternative to turn to if you run out of your regular food supplies. In addition, these are great alternatives to your 72-hour bag or even bug-out vehicle - that is, the bag of items that you would use to survive for the first 72 hours in an emergency and the vehicle that you would be using when driving out of some space where a disaster has occurred in.. You need to understand the different types of bars with which you can practice survival skills. However, these should not be the only items in your pantry at any given time. They should only act as backup during emergencies.

Water Supply

The importance of water for prolonged survival cannot be overstated. You must have water for you and your family to survive. It is prudent to have at least a two-week supply of water at hand. Also, a water filtration device that can be relied upon for prolonged disasters can be very helpful.

Rotating and resupplying

This is one of the most important practices that you will need to learn when running a food pantry. It is good to realize that all the items that have been brought to the food storage need to be used, rotated, and resupplied. This is the best way to have the freshest foods available in case a disaster strikes.

When you are organizing the food reserves, you should place the item that has the earliest expiration date in the front so that it can be used first. By doing this, you can incorporate the accounting policy of FIFO (first in, first out) in the operation of your food pantry. An inventory check needs to be done every six months to ensure that canned goods, preserves, and other storage items are all within their respective expiration dates.

To some, prepping is a passion, while for others it is one of the most efficient ways of keeping their families as safe as possible, especially in the event of emergencies. The above considerations, if kept in mind when purchasing food supply, will provide your family with a well-rounded food pantry that is stocked with a wide-ranging food supply, while at the same time assisting in promoting a healthy diet for all in times of disaster.

The Food Storage Process

It is important to have an emergency food pantry that ensures a consistent supply of food that your family can survive on in the event that a disaster cuts off normal access to food, water, and other utilities. An emergency food pantry that is well equipped is a necessity for every family. One point to note is that emergency foods should be non-perishable. They must not require cooking, refrigeration, or even water. It is up to you to determine the foods that you will stock in your pantry. It is critical to understand how to go about the whole process of starting up and getting your pantry ready just in case there might be emergencies in the future.

Plan for Your Pantry

Planning for your pantry is easier when you know how to get started, what you need to do, and what you need to buy. Preparing for a time when food is in short supply is not always an easy task and you can also rest assured that this is not one of the easiest things to think about. You can, however, equip yourself with the knowledge and skills you need in order to plan and build your home emergency pantry. By using all the information that is available to you, and applying that knowledge gained in the preparation process, you can efficiently stock your home pantry with the proper foods.

Location: The first step is to make sure that you have your long-term emergency pantry designed in a dry, cool, dark area. Many people choose basements, which are great. Large closets and garages are also good.

Available storage space: The next step is to measure and note the exact size of your available storage space. This should be done before you can decide on what to store. You should be realistic and determine exactly how much physical room you have to spare for food storage.

Layout: The last step is to lay out the space for access. It is good to plan where large stores of water will be put, where you will store cans, and where you'll store bins or boxes. After this, proceed to install the shelves appropriately.

Selection

Water: In the selection of items to stock, it is prudent to store water first. This is because the human body can survive weeks without food, but can only go for a few days without the intake of water. It is recommended to set aside a gallon of water per person for every single day.

If you are creating a long-term stockpile, this could take up a lot of space. You should therefore limit the amount of water that you will need to set aside by stockpiling water purification tablets, a gallon of bleach, or, if need be, a portable water purifier such as the ones that backpackers use.

Carbohydrates: You should then stock up on carbohydrates. In case of any crisis, you'll get most of your required calories through carbohydrates such as pasta, grains, and rice. It's best to buy in bulk quantities. It should be noted that carbohydrates account for about 50 to 60 percent of the foods people put in long-term storage.

Protein: The next category should be canned meat and beans. These are excellent and long-lasting sources of protein. At the same time, protein bars are also useful sources for protein and other essential dietary needs. You should expect protein sources to account for about 25 percent of the entire storage.

It is recommended that you supplement the storage with dried foods such as powdered eggs, dried milk, dehydrated vegetables, fruits, and ready-to-eat dehydrated meals. All these are ideal space-saving long-term food items. You will also need to include dried beans if space allows. These should take up less space than canned beans, though water will be required to cook them.

Supplementary items: Other items such as salt, garlic powder, pepper, and sweeteners should be set aside. Sweeteners could include sugar or any sugar substitute. Favorite spices should be included in the list. This is because tasteless food can sometimes be demoralizing, and can easily lead to a loss of appetite, which soon translates into malnutrition. Corn or olive oil for cooking and also flavoring food is great!

Utensils: The last step in selection is boxing up basic food preparation tools and utensils to store with emergency food supplies. You should ensure that you have the proper eating utensils, a can opener, and a cup.

It is good to remember to store a butane stove or gel-fuel with backups of cooking fuel. This will save you when you are not able to make use of any other sources of energy, which is a common scenario in the event of an emergency.

Stocking Process

Depending on the space available for your pantry, water needs to be placed in a large plastic drum with a pump, in gallon jugs, in five-gallon buckets, or in individual bottles. Whichever one of these alternatives best fits your needs should be applied.

In addition, loose bags of dried beans, rice, and vacuum-sealed packets of dried foods need to be in containers. They should be kept safe from insects and vermin by putting them in plastic or metal bins which have sealable lids.

Furthermore, jars and cans need to be organized on shelves, lined up by type with labels facing forward. This will help you with easy rotation. Rotation of foods in long-term storage should be done regularly as you buy new supplies. It keeps your long-term stores from spoiling. Expiration dates need to be routinely checked on your stored food and water. Any expired items should be thrown out.

Non-perishable foods that can be eaten without refrigeration, water, and cooking are great for emergency situations. You are free to pick any foods that your family likes. You can also consider including a few treats or any other comfort foods, which might help the family stay calm during the stressful time that comes after the emergency has struck.

It should not be forgotten that you need to stock enough food to feed your family for at least three days. If there are any pets, emergency food should be included for them as well.

At the same time, you may experience a few changes in your family in the course of the aftermath of the emergency; for instance, the addition of new family members or pets. Therefore, you need to regularly monitor and determine whether or not your emergency pantry is equipped to sustain the whole family in the event of a disaster. You need to discard or purchase items as new needs arise.

Must Have Foods for Your pantry

For any prepper, consistent stockpiling of nourishing and long-lasting food is an imperative priority. It means that the more individuals prep, the more secure they will be in any emergency or disaster situation. If you are searching for the right foods to store in your pantry for survival and sustenance before a crisis, here are some suggestions.

Purified and seltzer water

First and foremost, you need to have water in order to make it through the disaster. Therefore, as described above, you need to make plans to have some bottled water available.

Canned food

It's also a good idea to stock up on canned goods with high fluid content. Two good examples are canned pineapple juice and canned vegetable juice, which is easily accessible at your local market. These will provide both water and nutrition ions the body system.

Powdered milk

This type of milk can last for 2 to 10 years. You only need to add a bit of water in order to have a nutritious drink anytime of the day.

Hard cheeses packed in wax

It is not always easy to find waxed cheeses, but they are worth the effort. For example, sharp cheddar, Swiss, or parmesan in wax are extremely difficult to find. They last and also provide a great meal option.

Protein bars and protein drinks

As mentioned above, protein is a key source of energy for your daily nutrition. Canned protein drinks and protein bars last a long time, and they can be a key component of any pantry prepping strategy.

Dried and canned meats

This is another great source of protein. These meats are prepared to last. Examples of these are canned tuna, beef jerky, and chicken. A good stock of canned meat products is definitely critical for your prepping pantry.

Bouillon cubes, espresso coffee, and tea

These combinations provide nutrition for your drinking needs. Tea and coffee provide caffeine as well, which can be important for survival in the course of a disaster.

Bouillon cubes will provide you with a bit of a pick-me-up through a dense flavor with a small bit of sodium. Meanwhile, instant coffee and tea can be used to keep you awake with caffeine. You might want to have a bit of water with the coffee and tea though as they can dehydrate your body.

Oils

If you are going to do any kind of cooking, oil will be vital. Although most oils last one to two-years at most, you can consider coconut oil, which can last years before going bad.

Wheat flour

For many years, wheat has been a key diet constituent. It contains vitamins, fiber, some protein, and minerals. If you have access to water and also other basic cooking ingredients, then this product becomes a key baking ingredient even for the simplest meals.

Baby food

For many people, baby food and infant formula are expensive. In case you have a baby, boxed baby cereal and canned formula are easy to store and are also in great demand. They can serve as alternatives to those expensive brands for children's survival.

Fundamentals of Water Filtration

Water filtration is the process in which a contaminated water supply is prepared and made safe for human consumption. There are several methods of water filtration that can be used, but the main aim is to render the water fit for use through removing or killing bacteria, microbes, and other contaminants. The type of water filter that one can use depends mainly on the nature of the contaminants present in a particular water supply.

Purpose of Water Filtration

The main purpose of water filtration is to remove impurities from water. The designing of water filters is done in such a way that they can facilitate cleaner water from existing sources reliably and as quickly as possible. These filters provide safer water, improving the taste as well as removing bacteria that could otherwise cause infection or sickness if ingested.

Types of Water Filtration

As mentioned, there are several different forms of water filtration used. These include reverse osmosis, which condenses the water before forcing it through a semi-permeable membrane at high pressure. It then removes large particles such as bacteria. In addition, sand filters work similarly, though on a larger scale. They remove bacteria and large particle contaminants.

Another type is ultraviolet filters that bathe the water in radiation, thus killing bacteria. Activated carbon filtration reacts to the pollutants with carbon and removes them from the water, while distillation boils off the water, leaving pollutants behind.

Benefits of Water Filtration

There are many benefits that come from the water filtration process. Among these are the improvements to health. Research shows that filtering out chlorine from any drinking water reduces the risk of some cancers, such as colon and rectal cancer.

At the same time, by removing bacteria and other microbes from the water, the risk of disease is significantly reduced. This is particularly important for both children and the elderly, whose immune systems are not as strong, especially during emergency situations.

Water filters should be replaced on a regular basis to prevent a buildup of microbes and other contaminants. If this is not done, pollutants will build up. Once they reach a critical level, they can easily overflow into the water supply, making it more contaminated than before filtering took place. This should be considered especially during extended period of a disaster.

Importance of Food Stocking Your Pantry

In the beginning of the 19th century, most country homes had a walk-in pantry, as well as a root cellar, used for keeping fruits and vegetables. This pantry contained the essentials for the family's daily meals. However, times have changed. Today, people have walk-in closets to hang all their clothes, but no pantry!

Everyone needs to have a pantry that contains a good supply of the foods they use most frequently. In addition, a well-stocked pantry is not only the foundation for a good kitchen, but it is essential to a family's wellbeing, especially if some unforeseen calamity occurs. Two years' worth of food can be stashed away in the basement pantry. This food could come in handy even in the course of the first year in a new homestead. It is very essential, especially if you have a big family, which increases food demand.

Another very good reason to keep a well-stocked pantry is for convenience purposes. With a well-stocked pantry, you'll seldom need to run to the store to buy an ingredient for a meal. Everything that you will need is already available at home. Many foods, such as store-bought, flour, sugar, home-canned goods, rice, pasta, and dry beans, among others, can stay good for years with no special treatment, only keeping them dry, insect- and rodent-free, and relatively cool.

You may ask yourself where you should keep two years' worth of food and how you will be able to afford to buy that much. Others may claim that they are new to gardening, homesteading, and canning, and therefore fear that it will take them forever to fill their pantry. However, what you need to do is stock up on things when they are on sale. That way, you can save money.

At the same time, some of these are things that you get to do from time to time, so you do not need to worry about having to buy everything all at once. What you will need to do is to take some time and write down a list of the stuff you will need, and then from there you can proceed to buy the items slowly as you do your normal shopping over time.

In most cases, you should always buy more than one food item. If you need yeast, for instance, you should buy two one-pound bags, keeping one in a jar in the fridge to use now and freezing one for long-term storage. Again, you can buy a pound of yeast for only slightly more than a few packets of "regular" baking yeast at the store. This way, the cost is cheaper, and you will be assured of having plenty when you need it.

Keeping Pantry Food Safe and Tasty

There are four things that can cause food in your pantry to lose wholesomeness and flavor. They are:

- Moisture
- Extreme heat
- Insect infestation
- Rodents

While most stored foods will remain good for 10 years or longer (much more for canned goods) if stored in temperatures of 60ºF or less (but above freezing for canned goods), they can rapidly lose long-term storage ability when exposed to temperatures of 80ºF and higher. Therefore it's always best to keep your pantry cool, yet above freezing temperatures.

As with heat, moisture, either due to condensation, flooding, or a wet basement, can quickly turn your pantry into a sorry mess of molded and inedible food. In some homesteads, a pantry may be in an old basement. If it is very damp in the spring and winter, canning jar lids could begin to rust. You can solve the problem by using a wood stove to heat the pantry during the cold seasons such as winter (wood heat is quite drying), and ventilate it with a box fan during the spring and summer.

You can also install a sump pump with an automatic switch, which pumps out the excess water from the basement sump. Without this, it may overflow, wetting the basement floor, which greatly contributes to damp conditions in the pantry. By doing this, coupled with the wood heat and ventilation, you could have no more dampness in your pantry.

At the same time, given the smallest crack or hole, mice can and will get into the pantry, drawn by food smells, especially from foods that are not stored in stout containers. Foods such as flour, powdered sugar, cornmeal, and popcorn are huge temptations for rodents. They will quickly climb up onto shelves and chew holes in any available plastic or paper bags and gorge themselves on these foods.

Some go ahead and chew holes in jams and jellies when you use old jelly glasses topped with melted paraffin instead of more secure two-piece canning lids, helping themselves to your family's winter treats. To have them eat the food is bad enough, but they poop in it too, completely ruining the entire supply. They are impolite critters!

In addition, sometimes determined rodents will even chew through plastic storage containers to gain access to food. A mouse invasion in a year could make you lose a lot of food kept mostly in plastic ice-cream buckets or plastic gallon jars. It is good to remember that thinner plastic, such as that found in ice cream pails, can be easily chewed into, more so than heavy plastic like five-gallon buckets.

Another vital addition to a pantry is a set of good old-fashioned mouse traps. In the fall, you can "run a trap line" by setting several baited traps along the floor and any open shelves. You will also need to put as much effort as possible into shielding your house from rodent invasion.

All small cracks or holes should be closed up with caulking and spray insulation foam. Slowly, you will get rid of your mouse problem. Finally, a good, enthusiastic and effective hunting cat also helps to keep mice away.

Organizing the Pantry

A clean and organized pantry not only stores your food and kitchen items, but it makes meal time and preparation easy and less stressful. Utilizing all the space in your pantry gives you more work room in the kitchen to cook, bake, and enjoy time with family and friends. Cleanup will be simpler and easier when you know where each item should go. Learn how to make effective use of the storage space in your pantry to make your life easier.

Before you stock your pantry, remove everything that is in it. Wipe down the shelves with a damp cloth and sweep away debris. Use wet paper towels to scrub off food splatters from the walls inside the cupboard doors. This should be followed by checking products' dates. Any products past their expiration should be tossed. This gives you more room to see what you have to work with when dinnertime rolls around. In addition, you should invest in containers.

The next step is to choose transparent plastic containers to store everything from cereal to pasta. Make sure each container has a tight-fitting lid to protect your food from mold and bugs. You can consider additional shelving.

If your pantry is crammed full with various goods, consider taking out the present shelving unit and opting for one that utilizes the maximum amount of space in your cupboard. Slide-out shelves, stackable bins, and racks can help you get the most out of a limited space.

You should keep commonly used products close by and store rarely used foods at the back of your pantry. This makes for easy access when you are cooking. Items should be placed back in the same area. Your pantry needs to be kept in order by putting whatever is taken out back in its original spot, to help prevent you from going crazy while searching for an ingredient that may or may not be in the pantry.

In addition, when you want to optimize your pantry shelving, the first step is to take a look at what is there. For instance, you may have a lot of canned goods, spices, bottles, boxes, or bags. At the same time, you could be storing kitchen utensils in your pantry's shelves.

After taking stock of what the pantry has and what's stored on the shelves, it's now time to find pantry organizers to fit your needs. You can go to the store and visit the pantry organizer section. Let's say, for example, that you plan on keeping some spices for the long haul. You will need to use spice racks because they make it easier for you to see everything you need in a very easy manner. Either way, it is imperative that you select organizers that can fit in your shelves well.

If you store glasses on pantry shelves, then you can consider hanging a stemware rack underneath a shelf in order to utilize unused space. Again, the floor underneath the pantry shelving is a prime space. You can place a small hamper or two there to store bagged items like boxes of cereal or potato chips. This process helps in freeing pantry shelving for smaller materials.

Food Rotation in the Pantry

Rotating foods is essential to keep them from growing old. Though most foods in a pantry will stay fine for years, it's a good idea to rotate the food you are using so that the older foods can be used up first. This ensures that they don't get so old that they lose nutrition and flavor.

You need to periodically go through your pantry, moving the back jars/containers to the front, like they do in the grocery stores. It's really best if you jot down the year on the container. Many people are so busy that this doesn't get done.

However, if you write the year on the container or lid with a permanent marker, you will know exactly how old the food is and know which containers to use up first. You can bring the older containers of food upstairs to your little pantry, where it is real handy at mealtime. You get used to it much faster than if you have to go all the way downstairs to the big pantry to use it. Seeing it often reminds you to cook with it soon.

Through this, you might have already come to learn how much money you will save, how handy a pantry full of food is, and how good it feels knowing that you and yours will be able to eat properly because you will have properly stocked shelves. You can rest assured that this will be time and money appropriately spent.

In addition, you should be sure to check the expiration dates on all items that are purchased for your pantry. There is nothing worse than spending your hard-earned cash on a bunch of expired food. Thus, you should be careful when shopping at deep discount outlets since they tend to sell a lot of items that are very close to their expiration dates. This is not illegal, unfortunately, so just spend a little extra time and check the dates.

It is obvious that eating old food first and rotating the newer stock to the back is important in order to minimize wastage. It is okay to prepare your family's everyday meals from the stock of your emergency food pantry. What's the point in having a pantry full of food if you do not eat it?

That said, you need to be sure to replace what you use with newer food items. For instance, if you are preparing a can of beans for dinner, instinct tells us to eat the fresher things first, but you need to fight this impulse and grab the can that is expiring within the current year.

The next time you are at the market, you should grab a couple of cans to replace what you have already used.

Finally, most canned foods have a shelf life from three to four years, but this shelf life can be extended by the condition of your emergency food pantry.

Food Storage Methods

In most places, fruits and vegetables cannot be grown all year-round. However, storing food during the winter months from gardens or from farmers' markets allows you to maintain your commitment to local food all through the year. Before the advent of refrigerators and the long-distance transportation system, food storage techniques were essential for everyone.

Not too long ago, people and early pioneers were masters at subsisting on locally harvested food and were skilled food preservers. However, today, many have forgotten these skills. By learning how to preserve our own fresh, healthy food, we can save money and eat healthier at the same time!

Food can be preserved in a variety of ways specific to the type of fruits or vegetables you are trying to store. The main food storage methods include dehydrating, freezing, canning, jamming, cold storage, and pickling. These methods are presented below.

Freezing

Freezing is likely the most common food storage technique utilized today. Most produce requires blanching (heating vegetables in boiling water or with steam, then submerging them in ice water for cooling) before they are frozen. Blanching helps preserve color and nutrients in frozen veggies. Blanching time is specific to each type. A general rule is that when produce color intensifies, it is ready to be removed from the boiling water or steam. Peppers, tomatoes, onions and most fruits do not require blanching.

Winter squash should be cooked and then frozen. Fresh herbs can be chopped then frozen with water in ice-cube trays. You can also make pesto ahead of time and freeze it in ice-cube trays. After the ice-cube tray is frozen, remove the cubes and place them in a labeled freezer bag or airtight container. For tomatoes, cook into a sauce and then freeze. Some fruits will darken when frozen. This can be prevented by dipping fruit into an ascorbic acid syrup (or lemon juice) before freezing.

Frozen produce will generally last at least 12 months and oftentimes much longer. Always use airtight containers to prevent moisture loss and freezer burn. When freezing produce, like all other food storage methods, always save the best produce for storing, as it will stay fresh for longer and not go bad so easily.

Some advantages of freezing are that it is simple and retains much of the flavor and vitamins. The drawbacks are that freezing is energy-intensive. When the power goes out, for example during a storm, food will spoil if it gets warm. During a power outage, keep your refrigerator and freezer at its coldest by not opening the door unless absolutely necessary.

Dehydration

Drying food has some great advantages. Dried foods take up less space than frozen, canned, or stored produce. They are ideal for snacks, or to take on camping or hiking trips.

Also, if you're drying foods in the sun, this method uses the least amount of energy. Similar to other preservation methods, dehydrating fruits and vegetables slows down the chemical and microbiotic decomposition processes. Perhaps the oldest food preservation technique, dehydration can be accomplished using electric or solar-powered food dehydrators, ovens, and most simply, by laying food out to dry under the sun. Using electric dehydrators is the fastest method of drying vegetables and fruits, taking about six hours.

Peaches, apricots, plums, peppers, grapes, apples, bananas, currents, cherries, mangos, tomatoes, shell peas and beans are among the most popular fruits and vegetables to dry. Most vegetables need to be blanched before they are dried. You may want to dip fruit in an ascorbic acid syrup or lemon juice in order to preserve color.

You should chop the produce in uniform pieces for uniform drying rates. Vegetables and fruits can be eaten in their dry state, like raisins and apricots, or rehydrated for cooking, such as peppers. Dehydrated food will store from six to thirty-two months, depending on the type.

At the same time, shell varieties of peas and beans are the easiest to dry with no any special equipment. It is good to let pods dry out and become brown on the plants. You should pick pods before they crack and beans or peas fall out. If it looks like frost is imminent, pick the beans and peas and finish drying them off the plant. You should then freeze for two or three days to assure all bugs and their larva have been killed. They can then be stored in a jar in a cool, dry place for up to one year.

If you do not have an electric dehydrator, other simple drying methods that can be tried include hanging herbs and hot peppers to dry from their stems outside in the shade or even in a room with good circulation. Pepper should be stored in dry conditions for more than six months. In addition, you can also try laying out blanched tomatoes or apricots on cheesecloth stretched inside a wooden frame, and then covering them with another layer of cheesecloth in order to protect them against bugs. In most cases, drying takes two to four days.

Canning

Peppers, salsas, tomato sauces, tomatoes, pears, and peaches are the most commonly canned types of foods. Of all food preservation techniques, canning requires the most equipment and has the most specific process.

There are two main methods for canning; pressure canning for low acidity foods and water bath canning for high acidity foods, which should have a pH of 4.6 or lower. Boiling the jars both pressures canning and water bath and kills bacteria. Both methods of canning require large pots. For the latter, a pressure canner is preferable.

Canning jars, lids, rings, and jar lifter tongs are also used. In addition, for low acidity foods, a temperature of about 240°F, which is well above the boiling point, is required to kill any harmful microorganisms.

It is advisable to follow the safety precautions when canning in order to prevent food-borne diseases. If done properly, canning offers delicious home grown food all winter long. Canned foods should be stored at 50°-70°F in a dark and dry place.

Most of the farm produce from gardens will keep for a long period of time if harvested at the right time and stored correctly. It is important that vegetables and fruits should not be washed before they are stored. You should only store damage-free and mature vegetables.

Finally, it is critical to follow the humidity and temperature requirements. It is essential to keep things cool. You need to select a cool spot in your basement or other unheated space which does not freeze. A root cellar, which is not difficult to construct, is ideal.

Emergency Water Filtration Techniques

In any emergency water treatment, you should always filter water as a first step. If municipal water supplies falter or electrical power fails, you can turn to unusual sources. Serious illness can result from drinking water without filtering or treating available water from plumbing reservoirs, waterways, and swimming pools. In most cases, homemade filters or commercial filters do help to avoid these problems. There are different filters used which are discussed below:

Crude Filters

One of the real defenses against water-borne diseases is by boiling or chemically treating water. Filtration helps by removing many water contaminants. When the water is cloudy, it should be left to settle and then filtered through layers of a clean cloth. Some experts recommend boiling water for ten minutes. In addition, five to eight drops of chlorine bleach per gallon of water kills harmful viruses and bacteria, but crude filters only remove obvious debris in water.

Ceramic Filters

Ceramic water filters effectively remove harmful organisms, providing immediate drinkable water. They remove particles down to one micron in diameter. Not all filters in the market meet these standards. You should therefore check with the manufacturer to find out if additional steps may be needed. In emergency situations, filters which depend on a pressurized water system to operate will not be of great help.

Homemade Filters

The Homemade water filters which are built in stages do filter water in large amounts, though not perfectly. These filter stages should run from course to fine where first stages screen out large pieces of debris and later stages remove finer particles from water. In the last stage, the water could look clean if there is usage of a deep layer of activated charcoal. It should disinfected by with chemicals treatments or boiling before drinking it. Homemade filters are not considered enough to guarantee potable water, though they can be used in crisis.

Backpacking Filters

The use of small backpacking water filters are a great idea for the home emergency kit, although their total output can go as low as 200 gallons per filter. They are combined with simple cloth filters to remove coarse debris, producing drinkable water from emergency sources such as hot water heaters, or even from toilets' reservoirs.

Survival Filters

It is true that emergencies do not only happen in the cities but also in a wilderness situation when clean water runs short. In such situations, an emergency filter pit can be dug in the bank of a creek or even the shore of a lake. The ground itself is used as a primitive filter. Before filling a container, one should wait for the hole to fill and the water to clear. At this point, stage filters with found materials such as dry grass or clean sand can be rigged from spare clothing to serve the purpose

Pantry Checklist Summary

There are many sensible options for you to explore when it comes to getting different types of items that you might require when getting your survival plans ready. Here is a list of some of the many things that you might require when it comes to your general survival needs:

- Salt
- Raw honey
- Various hard grains including dry corn, buckwheat, millet and kamut
- Soft grains like quinoa, rye and barley
- Assorted beans
- Various flours
- Canned fruits, vegetables and meats
- Dried herbs
- Powdered milk
- Baking soda
- Apple cider vinegar
- Soaps

- Toilet paper
- Bandages
- Cleaning materials
- Charcoal and other items for setting fires for cooking purposes
- Medicine products

Prepper's Bug-Out Bag

The preppers' bug-out bag is the ultimate survival kit for anyone who is getting ready just in case disaster strikes unexpectedly. We never know when things will get out of hand, and it is for this reason that we need to be ready whenever we need to make a run for it. More often than not there is never enough time to gather things around, so having a bug-out bag does come in handy.

In the following pages, we are going to look at all the basic elements of the bug-out bag, from the reasons why you need to have one to making the good decisions on what to pack and bring along with you, as well as mistakes to avoid.

When you are planning your bug-out bag, you also have to plan for your family, especially the children. I have taken time to address these concerns, including security and communication measures that you should consider when you are bugging out with your family.

When disaster strikes, will you be ready? A prepper's bug-out bag is supposed to be the ultimate survival kit that will help you get as far away from a disaster situation as possible, while at the same time helping you survive the ordeal after the evacuation process is complete.

The primary purpose of the bag is to store supplies necessary for survival as you evacuate from a disaster. An elevated sense of caution is required to make sure that you can get to do this in the easiest way possible, without necessarily wasting time in the process.

Ultimately, you have to remember that in the event of a disaster, everything is at stake, and it can easily turn into a race for survival especially when you come across other evacuating parties along the way. The most important thing that you have to remember is that the safety of you and your family comes first, and everything else follows in line.

What Is the Bugout Bag?

Basically, your bug-out bag is your ultimate survival kit, the one thing that will house everything that you need to get you through whatever disaster situation you happen to find yourself in. The bug-out bag should help you think small. You know that you are not planning a holiday experience somewhere in the wild. You are trying to get as far away as possible from a disaster. When you are getting your bag ready, you need to remember that this is meant to carry only the things that you need.

The thing that you need to remember about the bug-out bag is that besides keeping all your basic, essential provisions in it, it is supposed to keep you going for at least three days, not a year, so plan accordingly when you are packing.

Why You Need a Bugout Bag

The Federal Emergency Management Agency (FEMA) is one of the main sources of legitimate and accurate information on the bug-out bag and one where preppers usually seek expert advice.

The bug-out bag is important, not just to you but to those you love. It is packed with necessities to help you to survive a disaster ordeal. Natural or otherwise, emergencies often strike without notice. This should be reason enough to get you planning for the worst case scenario. Imagine a situation where there is a chemical spill, and you need to evacuate immediately, or if there has been an earthquake, and you have to get as far away from the area as possible. How would you handle this situation?

Take some time and imagine if you were given 15 minutes to leave your house and vacate to safety. What would you carry? What would you leave behind? It is for this reason that you need to have a bug-out bag.

A bug-out bag is all about preparedness. This is not something that you are going to pack overnight and be ready to go. This is something that you should prepare many weeks or even months in advance. Preparing a bug-out bag ahead of time helps you carefully plan what you need to take. Also, updating the bag regularly keeps the contents relevant to your needs. It is all about making sure that you don't get caught unawares. When preparing the bag, you have to have in mind every room in the house. Every important aspect of the room must be taken into consideration so that you do not run the risk of leaving behind anything that you would find useful to you in the long run.

Get your Bug-Out Bag Not to Kill You!

In this section we are going to take a look at how to make the best use of the bug-out bag, and to make sure that it does not become much of a hassle. This is supposed to be a bag that is designed to give you everything that you need for at least 72 hours without weighing you down too much. This is also in consideration of the fact that a lot of people end up carrying more than they are supposed to, and in the process leave behind some important items

Purpose of the Bag

Theoretically, the bug-out bag is designed to provide you with everything that you need to make it through an ordeal for at least 72 hours outside your home before you get to any help. It is for this reason that the bag is supposed to be part of whatever plan that you have in place for disaster preparedness.

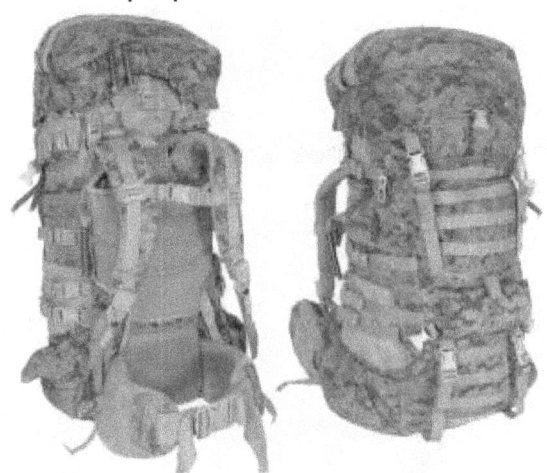

It's a common occurrence for people to throw in everything that they come across in the name of emergency packing. If you pack like this, I promise you that you will have too much to carry. It could slow you down way too much. The ultimate question in this scenario, therefore, should be what you NEED to survive, and not what you WANT to have with you when you are on the road.

Typically, the bug-out bag is supposed to carry you through about 72 hours, at least according to the FEMA recommendations. What you carry in your bag will vary from one person to another. As you prepare for this, remember that the choice of whether to bug out or to hunker down will be key in making the choice of what to carry in the bag.

The structure of the bag should be so that you can easily grab it and leave quickly. It should always be packed beforehand with all the supplies you need and be ready in a moment's notice. Also, you should have some prior practice on how to handle the bag so that you aren't surprised at how heavy it is. That way, you have time to consider what you might be able to leave behind.

At the bare minimum, the bag needs to have in it three of the most important things that you need in your life during such an ordeal; food, sufficient clothing, and a means of shelter.

Why You Need the Bag

One of the best questions that someone ever asked me was, "Do I really need the bug-out bag?" This is a very good question, and the answer to it will depend on the purpose for which you want the bag in the first place. There are two different types of these bags that are available in the market today. There is the kind of bag that you basically strap on to make your way into the woods, or the one you usually get when you want to take an adventure into some remote location with your friends for a retreat. This is a very good bag for those who plan to disappear into the forest until you are sure that the disaster has passed, and everything has eased up.

For a lot of people, the bug-out bag is more like a pre-packaged suitcase with all the things that they will need in an emergency. This is important because it allows them to leave quickly without having to waste time packing. This is a good type of bag for those who live in areas that are prone to disasters such as earthquake areas, hurricane areas, and flood-prone areas.

The good thing especially for those who live in such disaster-prone areas is that today there may be warnings beforehand about the possibility of disaster striking. As a result, you have more time to get your act together. Notwithstanding this, you have to make sure that you get yourself prepared beforehand to be ready for the challenge ahead.

How Your Bugout Bag Could Hurt You

Many people never give the bag much thought, and in the process they may pack more than they really need. The main concern here is the weight of the bag. Your bag is supposed to help you leave a dangerous situation, which means that it should help you get away as quickly and as far as possible. You will need to carry your emergency food supplies, medicine, shelter alternatives, and other necessities to get you through whatever situation you find yourself in.

In general, your bag needs to be between 1/3 and 1/4 of your overall body weight. Therefore, if you weigh 200 pounds, your bag needs to be around 50 pounds for you to carry it along easily. If you can make it lighter but still carry everything that you need, all the better.

Now that we know how much weight you are supposed to carry, let's move from the theory into reality. Think about it. Are you really ready and prepared to walk for three days straight with 50 pounds on your back? Remember that this is three days on perhaps different terrain, maybe rugged. If you have never imagined what this feels like, try thinking along the lines of carrying three gallons of water, the recommended amount of water that every individual needs. In the event that your bag is too heavy for you to carry around easily, it could certainly make you uncomfortable or even hurt you in the process.

The manner in which you pack your bag is another important factor for your consideration. If you pack your bag in the wrong way, it could create a distorted center of gravity for you. Distortion in the center of gravity will make your bag lean to one side and leave you off balance. Without proper balance, you will have little reasonable movement because you will be too tired to go far.

Think about it, what is your normal day schedule like? You probably go to work in the morning, come back in the evening feeling tired, eat, and go to sleep. You may not have the time to work out much. It is for this reason that you need to try and get some real exercise, and learn how to handle your bag appropriately.

Apart from the mistakes that you will make when packing your bag, the bag can also hurt you because of the attention that it can draw. In the event of a disaster, many people will be displaced from their homes. People may be desperate and in urgent need of the supplies that you carry. Let's call them hoarders for this reason.

Just because you have been intelligent enough to prepare your bug-out bag does not mean that everyone else shares the same level of sanity. There are those who see you packing and preparing your bug-out bag in the event of a disaster and think that you are paranoid. Once disaster strikes, they could, since they haven't prepared, resort to criminal activities to get by.

With this in mind, if you have a very large bag on your back, you are constantly a target. Remember that these individuals may also have kids who they need to take care of, so your package could seem like a very good way for them to keep their little ones alive.

But how do we get out of this mess?

Avoiding Near-Death Situations

Having looked at the mistakes that can make the bug-out bag a hazard, we now take a look at how to prevent such mistakes, and in the process, we learn how to make the best use of the bug-out bag. Solving the issue of being a moving target is very easy. You just need to be smart about how you go about packing.

Packing smart

When you are packing your bag, you have to remember that it is not a convenience store, but a life saver. There are a number of times when I have come across lists of things that people pack, and it makes me wonder what they really are planning to do. Once I saw a list that had fishing gear. I wondered whether the individual was going on a camping trip or if they were preparing to flee a disaster situation. Perhaps he/she had envisioned the possibility of having to chance upon a water body and make good use of some food. However, there's no guarantee that this water would be fresh and free of toxic chemicals in the event of a disaster. What this means is that the fish that you could get from it could be poisonous.

Remember, you are basically planning to stay on your feet for at least three days until things get better. Make sure that your bag contains all the important elements that you need, the BASIC elements. If you are lucky enough to pack all of these in the bag without reaching the weight limit for your body size, great!

There are those who plan to carry around things like their books or their Kindle to help them read and pass time. In the process of doing this, they tend to leave out important supplies. While it is important that you try to keep your mind occupied to avoid stress, at the same time, planning for a disaster means that you are planning for discomfort. With discomfort, the probability that you will come across a power source are minimal. Even if you do, there may be a lot of people already there trying to power their devices. To pass time, you need to think about other things like having conversations and trying to bond with those around you. The stronger the connections that you form with those near you during this time, the higher your chances of surviving.

Blending in

Just so you are aware, during disaster situations there are so many people feeling desperate, that even those who seem to be holding their own are scared of the uncertain deep within their hearts. Nobody knows for sure how long the disaster is going to persist and at the same time, no one knows what will happen an hour or a day from that moment on.

To be on the safe side, you should be able to blend in well with those who are around you. You have to learn to interact with people, learn to read the situation, and anticipate any sudden actions that might pose danger or situations that can be beneficial to you.

In as much as there is strength in numbers and an elevated sense of security, you should also take care to understand that when things get tough, you might actually need to know when to leave the pack behind and stay with your own.

Remember, it is all about SURVIVAL!

Your Bug-Out Bag Checklist

When you start writing your checklist when you are preparing your bug-out bag, a lot of people often run to the internet in search of an answer. There are a lot of ideas that you will find from people's experiences, from self-proclaimed experts and others. When you do this, you might end up with a very long list of supplies that you will need to get you through the ordeal. However, not everything in the list that you compile will be useful to you. When you think about it, everyone will compile their own list depending on their experiences and what they need. Situations differ from one person to the other.

You might actually end up with a very heavy bag with contents that you may not need. Instead, let's have a look at a very simple structure for your bug-out bag, a structure that will definitely help you build an efficient bag for you.

Essentials of the Bag

While there is much that you could pack in your bug-out bag, actually, you don't need to have a lot, just the bare necessities.

Water

This is the most important thing that you should plan for. You can survive for days on water alone even if you run out of food. You have to carry enough water with you because you can never be too sure about there being clean water wherever you go. However, in the event that your escape route runs along a good source of fresh water, you can replenish your supplies along the way. The most important thing to remember about water is that you must have <u>clean</u> water. Contracting waterborne diseases, particularly during an emergency, is not difficult. For the same reason, you have to be careful because there might not be any medical facilities around you. Clean water is a must.

Water bottle

When choosing your perfect water bottle, try and make sure that you get something that is durable but lightweight. Getting a water bottle that is durable is important. If it happens to fall, it should not crack or break and spill your water. There are different manufacturers today that have really awesome water bottles for such purposes, such as the Nalgene water bottle.

Filters

A water filter is necessary to help you get clean water. As mentioned earlier, you might find a source of water at some point on your way, but this does not necessarily mean that it will be water safe for drinking. You have to at least treat and filter the water before you drink it.

If you can gather rain water for, example, you cannot just drink it directly. This is where a good water filter will come in handy. There are those who will use UV pens, chlorine, or water treatment tablets for this purpose, but a good filter will also do just fine.

Besides, some of these elements need you to use batteries, which hopefully you've included in your bag. You'll also need a manual filter, something that will keep you going for days without worry.

Clothing and Shelter

Once you have your food and water in check, next you must consider clothing and shelter. Don't forget that our concern here is to get nothing but the basic needs for survival.

Clothing

This is supposed to be as simple as possible. Your choice of clothes should make it easier for you to survive once you have gotten away from the immediate dangerous situation. You will need to two pair of long pants, two long-sleeve shirts, two pair of socks, and two changes of underwear. For your long pants, you need to get very strong and durable options like denims. Also consider a pair of sweatpants if it's cold. If it's hot, still bring the jeans, but also bring some shorts. Although they leave a lot of your body exposed, it's also important to stay cool. Make sure you have enough cover to protect you from the sun, remembering too that much of that can be accomplished with sunscreen.

The biggest factor when it comes to selecting your clothes is to keep your choices as functional as possible. This is an evacuation situation, a disaster, and that's all you need to worry about.

You need protective covering of some type for your head. Pack at least a baseball cap. You'll also need a rain coat or poncho. Make sure that nothing is too heavy, or it could slow you down.

With shoes, be sure to pick the right kind. You need shoes that will allow you to walk for a very long time without having to worry about your feet. Your shoes need to be comfortable, sturdy, and most importantly, worn in enough to so that you can walk a long distance without feeling like throwing them away.

If you are evacuating during the cold season, don't forget to pack a pair of gloves.

Shelter

In an emergency, you're not looking for shelter that will be a replacement for a warm and welcome home, but if you chance upon one on your way, make do with it. In terms of shelter, you are looking for something to ward off the weather elements.

The most common choices that people make in this regard are usually from a tent to a simple tarp. Tents can be rather strenuous to carry with you. Besides, carrying a tent with you will probably be difficult and perhaps time-consuming to put up and tear down.

A simple lightweight tarp probably the best choice to keep you protected from the weather elements. The main aim here is staying alive, and at times this might come at the expense of living comfortably.

You might also carry a sleeping bag with you, but make sure that you get one that will be very easy for you to carry and will not take up a lot of space. Today you can get wonderful lightweight sleeping bags. Sleeping bags can cost you up to $500, but you can get an emergency sleeping kit for under $100. They are so light they can be folded to fit into your hands.

Survival Essentials

Children

Your bug-out bag is about survival; not just for you, but for your family too. If you have children, you have to plan in advance for them. You have to always be on the lookout for them and make sure that everything that works for you works for them too.

Assuming that your kids are coming with you, you must make sure that you pack bug-out bags for them too. These bags should be very light but carry the essentials that they will need along the way. As the adult, you have to plan for them, take the risks for them, monitor them, and know when they are struggling. The kids will likely be going through more stress than you but will probably not know how to deal it, or even have the words express their feelings.

Light and fire

When it comes to fire essentials, you need to be safe. Get disposable lighters, but make sure that you keep them in a waterproof bag. It is still important to have some backup. Carry a box of matches with you too. Some people choose to have lighters and firesteel as options and to ignore the matches. However, there are situations where you might not be able to start a fire anything but matches, so keep a box with you.

Insofar as putting up a source of light is concerned, headlamps are a great choice. One of the main reasons for this is that they are not only lightweight, but they are also awesome for kids. You do not run the risk of losing them, or have the inconvenience of having to carry it in your hands while juggling other things too.

For every member of the household, two headlamps would be great if you can carry them. When you are choosing the headlamps, you need to look at how efficient and effective they will be in your situation. You should use lamps that use AAA batteries. If you can get some that are rechargeable, even better.

Protection

As we mentioned earlier, the fact that you are carrying with you a well-stocked bug-out bag makes you stand out. Because of this reason, you need to have protective protocols in place. When you set out on your own, you can devise ways of survival to get you by very easily. However, when you are out there with your loved ones, you need to be able to protect them. Even when you are on your own, you still need to make sure that you have a means of protection. For a lot of people, carrying a gun is the ultimate go-to source of protection. There are different kinds of guns that you can pick for this purpose, but the most important thing is to ensure that your weapon is concealable, like a pistol. If your weapon is not concealable, anyone who notices you from afar can plan on how to take it from you and perhaps use it against you.

One more thing, keep the weapons away from the kids!

Communication

For communication, you may see suggestions that you get military grade or limited range radios. If you feel that's necessary, OK. This is important, especially if you are travelling in a large group of people, and you need to stay connected to one another. However, simply staying close to one another is really the best communication equipment you can get.

For your phones, you should have a way to charge them. Solar chargers are best. Walkie-talkies can come in handy too. If you are getting special communication equipment, teach your family how to use them before an emergency strikes. You can learn, go through the tutorials, and try them out so that you all know what to do. It would be useless to have the terrific communication equipment and not know how to use it in the event of a disaster situation.

Useful tools

Since we have probably covered almost everything that you will need as essentials, how about some general tools that you should not leave behind?

A good pocket knife will save you a lot of trouble, so make sure you have one with you – and remember to keep it concealed and safe so that you do not harm yourself or anyone around you with it accidentally.

A pair of pliers is such a good multi-use tool and is always good to have with you. They are very handy and will definitely be useful. There are times when you can have them double up as hammers for small nails.

You will need something to boil water and to cook with like a lightweight pot. You'll also need a first aid kit. A good first aid kit is not one that will allow you to perform a successful surgical operation, but one that allows you to take care of some of the basics, like dressing a wound.

Hygiene

Just because things are tough and you are out in the wild does not mean that you need to forget about hygiene. By maintaining proper hygiene, you will be able to ward off some communicable illnesses. In your bug-out bag, make sure that you have some soap, toothpaste, toothbrush, floss, hand sanitizer, sunscreen, and any small elements that will help you.

For the ladies, you'll need tampons and/or maxi pads. You will not need your makeup. You might have to camouflage yourself in mud for protective purposes from time to time. You never know what nature will throw your way.

Duct tape – never forget to carry this with you. It's good for almost everything!

Bandanas come in handy for many reasons, and not just for covering your head. They can also be wrapped around a wound or act as an arm sling.

Spare batteries should absolutely be on your list.

Also, carry with you some form of identification. You never know when this will come in handy.

Navigation

Together with your plan, it is equally important to make sure that you get the proper navigation equipment to keep you on course. You should have a detailed map with you. For those with smartphones, the temptation to use Google Maps will be there, but I can guarantee you that without a good network connection, Google Maps will only get you so far. If you run out of batteries, you run out of luck.

You must know how to read a map, use a compass, and give and use directions. In the event that there is a pre-arranged location where you are supposed to meet others, make sure that you have at least three routes to get to these locations just in case any of them is impassable.

For those who constantly go on hikes in such areas, try and mark the common spots such as streams, presence of wildlife, and so forth on your map so that you have an easier time finding them.

Identification and money

One other thing, though this might not really sound like being so high up on the list for a lot of people, try to carry with you some form of identification. You never know when this will come in handy.

Make sure that you have with you your identification cards, social security cards, birth certificates and any other form of identification especially for your children. These must be kept very carefully.

As you make your plans for evacuating in the event of an emergency, take your time and spare some money aside for this purpose. Always make sure that the money that you have set aside is in currency denominations that are small enough so that you do not have trouble finding smaller denominations when you are in need.

There is no limit to the amount of money that you can set aside for this as long as you are sure that what you set aside will be able to help you get through the toughest times.

Common Bug-Out Bag Mistakes You Need to Avoid

The bug-out bag is important to anyone who is keen on preparedness. It is an important element that you cannot take for granted when things get tough and disaster strikes. Take your time to learn all you can about preparedness, reading books and blogs, and watching TV shows about how to be prepared.

If you have to leave your home during a disaster, you may not know when you can come back. Because of this, if you make some mistakes in preparing your bug-out bag, you could be in a lot of trouble. Here are some of the most common mistakes people make with bug-out bags.

Picking the Bag Haphazardly

You need to spend some time and select your bug-out bag carefully. This bag could be your lifeline for a number of days. There are a lot of people who often look at bug-out bags that they find on websites and decide to purchase them just because they think they look awesome. No.

To be precise, there was a time when I was checking out a bug-out bag that was being reviewed on a particular website that I used to frequent. This bag was hyped as a military-type bag, and indeed it seemed to have a lot of room in it. With a lot of room and the military concept behind the bag, I was totally hooked on it, considering that these are guys who basically spend a lot of time on the road, so it sounded like a good buy. Besides, the bag looked cool to me too.

I immediately made an order. When I got the bag, it was just as I had hoped for, with all the cool compartments. On the other hand, the bag weighed close to six pounds without anything inside. How was I going to carry this after packing in all the stuff that I wanted with my small size? Luckily, I happened to know someone big enough who could make some good use out of it.

So, what did I learn here? When you want to purchase a bug-out bag, it is important to ensure that you try it out before you place an order. While today we are fascinated with shopping online, when it comes to your bug-out bag, take your time and purchase it in a store. Try it out, make sure it fits and will be functional, and then you can take it home.

Before you purchase the bag, go to stores where these bags are sold, like an academy or any sports store that stock such. Speak to their salespersons and tell them what you need. Take your time and find a bag that fits your size, your shape, your physique, and that will not become a bother for you when you are using it.

To know if the size will be perfect for you, try inserting some weights in it to see if it really is manageable. Try and walk around in the bag for at least 10 or 20 minutes inside the store and determine whether it will be comfortable for you. Remember that those 20 minutes are crucial to you since you could be carrying the bag for days.

Eventually, I managed to find one bag that was just perfect for me, but I can guarantee you that I had to be very patient to find what I wanted.

The Attention Seeker Bug-out Bag

I always thought people with esteem issues were the ones who were attention seekers until I came across particular bug-out bags that did just that. From my experience, you need a bag that does not really attract unnecessary attention. Of particular note is the color of the bag. You need not pick a bag with screaming colors. You don't want to get all the wrong attention directed towards you. If yours has bright colors, you may have just turned yourself into an easy target.

To avoid this, always go for the dark and plain-colored bags, with careful choices in navy, black, grey, or khaki-colored bags. At the same time, focus on the design of the bag. Make sure that it is not too fancy. In such a situation, you should be looking for something functional rather than fashionable.

When packing, always try not to pack anything outside the bag, especially anything that chimes or jingles, because this could attract the attention of not only people who are looking to pilfer the contents of your bug-out bag, but animal predators that might also lie in wait.

The Water Question

As we said earlier, when it comes to survival outside your home in the event of a disaster, water is at the top of the list of what you'll need. You have to carry enough water to get you from one point to another. Packing water purifiers and iodine tablets to use in case you come across a source of water that might be contaminated are also a must. However, what happens if you never come across a source of water? Always make sure that you carry with you as much water as you could possibly need.

Overloading the Bag

A lot of people make the mistake of panic packing their bug-out bag. You have to know how much weight is enough for you to tug along, and what should be in the bag.

The highest amount of weight recommended for you to tug along should be on the higher side of a quarter or a third of your weight. However, a third of one's weight is an extreme measure for those who are built for this kind of thing. Taking into consideration the fact that not everyone has the build for it, hauling around a third of your weight through rugged terrain and a lot of other hazardous conditions is not easy.

When you are packing, you need to remember the real possibility of walking through dangerous conditions, of having to run for your life, or even of having to stay still and wait for some dangerous situation to pass before you can proceed on your journey. As has been said in the past, always prepare for the worst, but hope for the best.

Forgetting the Children's Bug-out Bag

It is understandable that you will end up packing a lot of supplies for your children inside your bug-out bag, but at the same time, consider packing some supplies for them in their own bags that they can carry with them. This will include things like snacks, small toys, or anything that can make them comfortable.

The best thing about this is that by carrying their own bags, it will have eased enough space on yours to carry other useful stuff that you will need on your way. You should, of course, not overload your kids' bags because this will only slow down your journey, and give you twice the challenge you are trying to avoid.

Keep in Shape

Keeping in shape is vital when planning for disaster situations. Once when I was walking down the street, I happened to chance upon some guy pacing on the sidewalk very early in the morning with a big backpack. I wondered what he was doing, considering that the weather was fine, and there had been no disasters reported on the news for a very long time.

However, since I was an early morning jogger, I had the chance to meet him again a couple more times. The third time I met him, I mustered up some courage and asked him what he was doing. He told me he was just getting in shape for a backpacking trip that he had been planning in a few months. That was when it hit me! What a brilliant idea! Getting in shape before an emergency is only common sense. While I can understand that having to do the whole exercise with the bag on one's back might be a tall order, you can do some exercises which will help you get into shape and be ready for your potential emergency.

Repairing Your Bag

In the course of your journey, you may come across different terrains, different weather conditions, and many other factors that could rip your bag. For this purpose, you should have a sewing kit with you to take care of any tear that might happen. You need a small, heavy duty sewing kit. Some are available that can double as suturing needles. If you don't carry anything to help with repairing the bag, you could lose some of the contents of your bag along the way, or have to carry the bag on one arm if one of the straps lets go. The bag is supposed to be conveniently strapped around your shoulders, and any other position would change the convenience and comfort levels of carrying it around, which in turn will slow you down.

Familiarity with the Bag Contents

If you are the kind of person who packs their bags a long advance, be sure to check through the contents from time to time. You need to know what is important and what is not. You have to check the packed clothing to ensure that they fit in with whichever season that you are planning for, and for the kids, that they still fit.

There are contents of your bag that may have either dried, expired, or leaked. These need be thrown away. When you are organizing your bag, you have to be familiar with the contents so you don't leave anything to chance. This also helps you to find something in the bag.

Sharp Objects

Always make sure that all the sharp objects that you are carrying with you are properly covered. This means that you should have the right kind of protection for things like knives, axes, or machetes.

Besides the fact that they could cause an injury, they could become a weapon against you. Even in your hands they could become a hazard if an accident occurs. If not properly concealed, they can harm you, or tear your bag, something that you definitely must avoid.

Last Minute Packing

Last-minute packing is one of the worst things you can do. You must not wait until there is a disaster for you to start emergency packing. That's the prefect recipe for mistakes. You are much more likely to leave important things behind and instead carry with you a lot of unnecessary items.

There is a good reason why we call this preparedness. It's to get you ready in case disaster strikes. It is important that you get your things perfectly inventoried to ensure that you know where everything is.

Planned Escape Route

When you are planning the route, you need to consider the following important factors:

- Consider where you are starting your journey from and where you are heading to
- Consider the person that you are taking with you on the journey
- Consider the mode of transportation that you will be using on the route
- Consider the equipment or anything else that you will have to carry or bring along with you

That being said, there are important tools that you must have to get through or to use the bug-out route as desired. These are:

- A compass
- Water
- Pen and paper to document notable things you come across along the way

- Communication equipment

Finally, once you have all of these in check, you need to plan for the route assessment. Route assessment is all about being familiar with the route, and making sure that you are comfortable with it, and any other alternatives that are available.

For a proper route assessment you need to do the following:
- Familiarize yourself with the area
- Look for any possible routes that can be used as alternatives and from there prioritize them
- Make sure that the alternative routes have been documented on the map

Take some time and run through all the routes to know them well enough.

With these tips you should be able to make your way out of any situation, and get you and your family to safety. Don't forget to practice your escape route with your bug-out bag packed. Involve everyone that will be coming with you. Being prepared is much safer than panicking in the face of adversity.

Quick Reference Checklist for your Bug-Out Bag

The following is a simple checklist that can help you plan for the things that you will need for your bug-out experience:

- Waterproof tent or tarp
- Dehydrated meals
- Sleeping bag (ultra-light)
- Mosquito net shelter
- Water filter & bottle
- Water bottle
- Solar water collection bags
- Map compass
- Survival knife
- Fire starter
- Can opener
- Machete
- Flashlight
- First aid kit
- Sunscreen
- Road maps
- Topographical maps
- Firearms if necessary
- Antibacterial soap
- Reading/sunglasses
- Transistor radio
- Nose and mouth mask
- Extra clothing
- Duct tape
- Drinking water

- Source of heat
- Insect repellant
- Wet napkins
- Hand sanitizer
- Travel toilet paper
- LED headlamps
- Money in small bills
- Emergency whistle
- Bandana
- Binoculars
- Face paint
- Resealable bags

Photography Credits

http://4.bp.blogspot.com/-
0xmDYliPGGw/TjLsxgw3e7I/AAAAAAAAAHg/h2UVrK3XBTQ/s1600/faultline.jpg

http://static2.skapiec.pl/11179585-1-1-5-td-kierunek-do-wyjzncia-drogi-
ewakuacyjnej-w-prawo.jpg

http://www.worldmapsonline.com/images/globe_turner/states/geonova_north_caroli
na_state_lg.jpg

http://www.pure-pro.com/images/020804.jpg

http://www.isotrek.com/image/cache/data/katadyn-mybottle-portable-water-
purification-system-700x700.jpg

http://realgoods.com/media/catalog/product/cache/1/image/9df78eab33525d08d6e
5fb8d27136e95/r/1/r12841-2.jpg

http://melissaknorris.com/wp-content/uploads/2012/08/Pressure-Cooker-Loaded-
with-Beans.jpg

http://cdn1.production.liputan6.static6.com/medias/678919/big/three-year-pizza-
army-mre-field-ration-4.jpg?t=1999306632

http://www.ecchanoi.gov.vn/UploadCute/denpin11_1.jpg

http://ecx.images-amazon.com/images/I/61OLRxKTZNL._SL1100_.jpg

http://media-cache-
ak0.pinimg.com/736x/bf/90/2b/bf902bbd389d6458289752d8e87aef6a.jpg

http://ecx.images-amazon.com/images/I/712AUYH6fcL._SL1500_.jpg

http://www.topsurvivalweapons.com/wp-content/uploads/2015/01/best-survival-
backpack.jpg

http://3.bp.blogspot.com/-
_a8TzulUufA/Thq99FkqYZI/AAAAAAAAFoY/aOOPJ_HZPPA/s1600/%25E0%25B8
%2595%25E0%25B8%25B0%25E0%25B9%2581%25E0%25B8%2581%25E0%2
5B8%25A3%25E0%25B8%25875.jpg

http://lh3.googleusercontent.com/-
fLOEKZ7KcNc/UDliz3nUE6I/AAAAAAAADds/JUuYr3sCpiU/s1024/African_Garden
s_Lesotho_keyhole_garden_above.JPG

187

https://s-media-cache-ak0.pinimg.com/736x/4a/5a/3b/4a5a3b93d7a27c20d97c0dbfb783b9b2.jpg

http://4.bp.blogspot.com/-hLpqHHdxR-0/UPmv63aZipI/AAAAAAAAB6A/5MWMBvmiQEQ/s1600/UVI_aquaponic_plant_production.jpg

https://24-7news.dk/wp-content/uploads/2014/10/alarmsystem.jpg

https://upload.wikimedia.org/wikipedia/commons/a/ac/Security_camera_%281%29.jpg

http://www.alyx.com/stranger/wp-content/themes/vistered-little-1/wallpapers/wallpaper12.jpg

http://s2emagst.akamaized.net/products/562/561155/images/res_b0346756ef4d2667aae91592c99142ad_full.jpg

http://www.supreme-maintenance.com/wp-content/uploads/2013/12/solar_panel_185692.jpg

http://intramar.nl/wp-content/themes/ihitro/costum/front-end/site-img/1b.png

http://www.dhresource.com/albu_262202929_00-1.600x600/tragbare-gewerbe-medical-k-hlschrank-gefrierschrank.jpg

http://www.shoplivart.com/media/catalog/product/cache/1/image/9df78eab33525d08d6e5fb8d27136e95/l/m/lms-2500_1a.jpg

http://www.quickanddirtytips.com/sites/default/files/styles/insert_large/public/images/3732/groupplasticbottlesofwater.jpg?itok=egSwsrMR

https://upload.wikimedia.org/wikipedia/commons/thumb/0/01/Sawdust_composting_toilet.jpg/1024px-Sawdust_composting_toilet.jpg

http://kentsmini.com/site/images/washtub-washboard.jpg

http://orenix.com/WebRoot/StoreFR/Shops/eb2192/MediaGallery/Telephone_Satellite/Thuraya/Thuraya_Phone-4W.JPG

http://lh3.ggpht.com/-JJQJHs1CpvE/UXciQwn4D6I/AAAAAAAAJic/dvuxZit0uT8/Weather%252520Radio_thumb%25255B5%25255D.jpg?imgmax=800

http://kresala.eu/wp-content/uploads/CB-Radio.jpg

http://mla-s2-p.mlstatic.com/mascara-de-gas-israeli-504201-MLA20292547888_052015-F.jpg

http://www.pooltablesni.com/images/pool-table-images/fold-away-l.jpg

http://reach-unlimited.com/_img/xlqe1tfknx8bawkmympaevadgjadj9.jpg

http://1.bp.blogspot.com/_-E5BrbUrG8U/TOBrkNK-h2I/AAAAAAAAAKI/u8Vk5fQrQDw/s1600/IMG_0515.JPG

http://survival-mastery.com/wp-content/uploads/2015/04/Food-in-the-jars.jpg

http://3.bp.blogspot.com/-J3Md8jaJM6M/Toal4uD6ogI/AAAAAAAAC50/mldcmRYqQzs/s1600/IMG_4830.JPG

http://thehappyguy.com/wp-content/uploads/2011/05/foodcans.jpg

http://www.milwaukeewaterfiltration.com/wp-content/uploads/2013/03/Office-Water-Filtration-Milwaukee.jpg

http://ecx.images-amazon.com/images/I/61UD2TnZBLL._SL1000_.jpg

http://www.theprepperjournal.com/wp-content/uploads/2013/09/BugOutBag.jpg

http://realarmygear.com/wp-content/uploads/2013/10/USMC_ILBE_lg-11.jpg

http://survivallife.com/wp-content/uploads/2013/10/heavybackpackfeat.jpg

http://www.thesurvivalistblog.net/wp-content/uploads/2014/07/IMG_09431.jpg

http://suburbansurvivalblog.com/wp-content/uploads/2010/10/tent.jpg

http://www.caminhodesantiago.com.br/images/duvida_que_levar.jpg

http://bug-outbagmethod.com/images/survival-gear/knives/Survival-Knives.jpg

Parting Shots

It is widely known that readiness is a great virtue. However, not everyone has turned that knowledge into deeds yet. I hope that you've found out everything you needed about being a prepper. Now, you are able to live on without having to fret in case a disaster of any kind befalls your family, city or even country.

Preparedness is key to surviving disasters and other emergencies and it's never too early to start preparing. With the right things in the right places, you should not have much to worry about. Always try to be ready ahead of schedule.

www.ingramcontent.com/pod-product-compliance
Lightning Source LLC
Chambersburg PA
CBHW062159280526
45788CB00001B/366